America's Best Town

(Bluffton, Ohio 45817)

By
"Average Joe" Schriner

Llumina Press

ISBN: 1-932303-24-3
Printed in the United States of America

Table of contents

Dedication
Special thanks
Introduction…   1
Social Health of a Town   5
"The air we breathe"   7
Bluffton Hero   11
The Big Orange Chair   13
Et Cetera Shop   17
Common Grounds   21
Community   23
Brush Strokes (Painter's Plus)   27
It's better to give…   29
Minimalism Musings (Painter's Plus)   35
Global Bluffton   37
Restaurant Hopping, Bluffton Style   43
Blaze of Lights   47
Speaking Out, Bluffton Style   51
"Big Roger"   57
'Buy Bluffton'   61
An 'Unlightened' America   67
Marching to a dift. Oboist (Painter's Plus)   71
'Beeutiful' Music (Not)   73
'Wood' that there be art   77
Free air all around!   81
Bluffton 'learns to like dandelions'   83
Bluffton Globetrotter   87
"Put me in coach…"   91
Another 'different' type of Bluffton doctor   103
The food we eat…   105
'World Walking,' Hugh Downs Style   113
Running Dog With Monkey   121
A 'weird something' (Painter's Plus)   125

An outlet for their youth   127
Bluffton Family Recreation   131
"Only have a cardboard box."   137
The 'Big Blue Penguin'   141
Public Enemy #1   145
Historical Society, and a 'Wisp of a Yodel'   149
Bluffton seniors   151
'Quality of Death'   155
Highlander Grogg and 'That's All Folks…'   157
"Eat a Peach" (Painter's Plus)   163
End Note(s)   169
About the author   173
Order form   174

Dedication

This is dedicated to everyone in Bluffton, Ohio 45817, who work to make the town what it is.

Special thanks to:

God, who seems to continually smile on Bluffton. Liz for sharing the "Bluffton experience" with me. Sarah and Joseph for continuing to be the "bestest" kids. Matt Meyer for believing in us, the vision, and for all the stuff you do behind the scenes.

The staff at Bluffton College's Musselman Library: Paul Weaver for all the archives help – and opening the door that one day. Carrie Phillips for *all* the expert technical assistance. Mary Jean Johnson for running the "best" library in the country. And also to Kathleen Aufderhaar, Barb Easterday, Ann Hilty, Karyl Crawford… for all the other reference help, etc.

Bluffton College in general (administration, professors, students…) for contributing to BC being more than just a "college," but rather an expression of some pretty inspiring faith.

BC English Professor Lamar Nisly for the supirb editing help. (Did I spell 'supirb' right Lamar?)

Dale Way for the friendship, the help and the "Painter's Plus Moments."

Cindy, Dan, Adam and Aaron Basinger, who are all: "determined, enthusiastic, polite…"

Wendy and Andy Chappell-Dick for all the community-building work.

First Mennonite Church for your creativity in living out the gospel message.

Mark Schumacher for (bravely) driving the van.

"Ms. Doreen" and "Ms. Diane," and the rest of the cafeteria staff at Blanchard Valley Hospital, for the morning smiles, and of course: *the muffins.*

Bill Keeney for the lantern.

Ron Rich for the insight into "light pollution" -- and the guts to fight it.

The Bluffton Public Library staff (Martha, Gail, Cheryl, Lisa, Terri, Carolyn, Sondra, Svetlana, Brian, Ross...) for your professionalism and congeniality – however, your inability to keep Dave Baumgartner out of the facility has been a little troubling.

Dave Baumgartner for being a "little troubling" – although a good music reviewer and even better neighbor.

Everett Collier and the staff at the Bluffton Post Office for letting me "loiter."

Mitch Kingsley for your town vision, although your choice of bicycle seats is a little suspect.

Royce Engle for the candle.

Terry Chappell for the diagnosis.

The 6 a.m. basketball crew.

Tim Stried and Steve Schenk for the pictures.

Common Grounds for the coffee, *all* the coffee.

And lest I forget: the Bluffton Beaver.

And if I've forgotten anyone, to you too.

Introduction

Bluffton, Ohio 45817.

For its rather small population, 3,877, it's been the residence of an inordinate number of famous people.

It boasts of once being the home of one of the nation's most popular comedians. One of the top American television journalists, ever, lived here. A doctor who recently became an international hero lived in Bluffton. One of the best Professional Football League players of his day resided here.

Even the most notorious criminal of all time (or at least during the early '30s) stopped here – albeit quite briefly, guns blazing.

What's more, in a saga that would rival the story the movie *Hoosiers* was based on, a small, rag-tag Bluffton High School girl's basketball team did what seemed the impossible: they won state – in a most unusual way.

Bluffton also has a business that's practically a one-of-a-kind in America.

It has one of the best colleges in the country, although a questionable mascot.

And if all that isn't enough, it is even the home of a presidential candidate.

Carmel, California it ain't.

I, by the way, am the presidential candidate.

During Election 2000, and now for Election 2004, I have campaigned extensively. Known as "average Joe," I travel the country with my wife (and campaign manager) Liz and our two children in a small motor home.

Our story, so far, has appeared in some 400 small to intermediate size newspapers, about 100 regional network TV news shows, a lot of radio... and Bluffton College reference librarian Paul Weaver just recently mentioned us in his family's Christmas newsletter.

Who needs CNN, huh?

In the ilk of Charles Kuralt, I have also been a journalist who has traveled the "back roads of America" quite extensively as well.

In all this traveling, I've seen a tremendous amount of towns.

And of all these towns, the one that I find to be the best is: Bluffton, Ohio.

Now when I say "best," I don't mean things like most scenic. Bluffton is billiard table flat and has corn, a lot of corn. And I don't mean most affluent. Carmel, California, it ain't. I don't even mean tourist Mecca. Greg's Pharmacy here has, at best, three different postcards.

What I do mean by best, is that Bluffton has the best "quality of life" of any small town I've seen.

Call it serendipity, say it's fate, acknowledge even a few people might have simply run out of gas, and money, on I-75 on the outskirts here... But whatever the reason, a unique group of people have seemed to assemble in Bluffton, *with a mission.*

Started to Run

I had initially come here in the Fall of 1973 to go to Bluffton College as a freshman. At the time, I wasn't exactly looking for deep "quality of life" stuff.

I was looking more for a girlfriend, some "good times," and a college major – in that order.

After a year at BC, I hadn't found a girlfriend, the "good times," the way I saw "good times," hadn't been many (Bluffton is a Mennonite college), but I had found a major: journalism.

At the time, Bluffton College didn't have a journalism major. So I left.

I eventually graduated from Ohio's Bowling Green State University with a journalism degree, then started to research America.

Along the way, I started finding these marvelous people working on all sorts of projects to enhance their town's quality of life. And along this path, I began to see quality of life was more than just a woman (my wife Liz not withstanding), "good times," and so on.

True quality of life seemed more about the depth of family life, the health of your natural environment, the degree of town community-building…

After awhile, and *a lot* of miles, I started to think these common-sense, small town people behind these small town quality of life projects should be in D.C., inspiring a nation.

So I started to run.

For president.

Of the United States.

Of America.

My first run was in Campaign 2000. We traveled 20,000 miles over 19 months, campaigning in all 48 states in the Continental U.S.

We lost.

Our three-year-old Joseph kept sticking his tongue out at people during the speeches.

An Oz

In an attempt to regroup prior to running again, Liz and I started to think about small Ohio towns our family could settle in that had some of this quality of life stuff our platform was all about.

Bluffton came to mind.

At a conference where I'd given a speech during

Campaign 2000, I'd met Wendy and Andy Chappel-Dick, who, as coincidence would have it, were from Bluffton. And when we called, they graciously offered to give us a tour.

We liked what we saw at first glance, and, after 28 years, I moved back to Bluffton, this time with a family.

Now basically what I expected from Bluffton was a quiet haven with a relatively nice sense of community, a good hardware store (small towns always have good hardware stores) and the off chance that the town coffee shop, I do a lot of writing in coffee shops, might have a flavor, or two, other than the Regular blend.

However, what I walked into was something more. A *whole* lot more.

Bluffton was a 'diamond,' if you will, sitting in the middle of the cornfield. A real *Field of Dreams*. An Oz.

And I'm not just saying that because I discovered the coffee shop did, in fact, have a Hazelnut blend…

Chapter 1

Social Health of a Town

Getting to Bluffton, we moved to a small home on Lawn Ave., right next to the elementary school playground – a drawing card for our kids.

In the first week, I was out one day playing tag with our children, Joseph, 4, and Sarah, 6, for a good 20 minutes. Then I ran out of gas. It happens.

I sidled up to another father, who too had apparently run out of gas and was sitting under a tree. Jeff Gingerich had come this day with his three-year-old daughter Katie.

Jeff and I commiserated about 'running out of gas,' then went on to talk about kids, the neighborhood, the weather and a constellation of underlying factors that drive group behavior in the United States. *(Well, you can only talk about the weather so long, huh?)*

Jeff, I found, is a professor of sociology at Bluffton College. He told me he teaches students in a sort of 'outside the lines' fashion about how to view the world.

Being an independent presidential candidate, I told Jeff I'd grown quite accustomed to being considered, oh, 'outside the lines' a bit myself, and I'd be fascinated to hear more of his thoughts on America.

Who's measuring that?

Several days later, I was in Professor Gingerich's office on the 3rd floor of Bluffton College's Centennial Hall.

Jeff said in one of the first classes every semester he explains to students we have economic indicators for practically everything in America.

We know how many people are employed, unemployed.

We know if a person makes so much a year they are: lower middle class, or upper lower class, or *some* class.

Also, in a computer somewhere, there's consumer data showing what someone's last three car purchases were. The data will also show if that someone is in debt, with a detailed analysis of who they are in debt too, and for how much. The data will even show if that person is starting to increase their shopping on the Internet, with a breakdown of what kind of items they are buying.

But what about the amount of quality time someone is spending with their kids? Jeff asks his students. To what degree is that person trying to help the environment, build community, be involved with civic projects, or is out volunteering to help the poor?

Who's measuring that? Should we be measuring that?

As it applies to individuals. As it applies to towns. As it applies to the nation.

Jeff believes America should be putting a lot more energy into detailing and measuring these types of "quality of life" factors. In fact, one of the professor's class texts, *The Social Health of the Nation*, proposes there should be an annual "National Social Survey" that tries to get an ongoing feel for these other types of issues.

While there are versions of this type of "National Social Survey" in 15 European countries to date, there is, unfortunately, no similar formal survey in America.

So I decided I'd do an 'informal one,' not on the whole U.S. (our campaign vehicle is a rather slow '74 conversion van), but on Bluffton.

And the following is the "quality of life" dynamics, and a whole bunch of other stuff, I observed.

Chapter 2

"The Air We Breathe"

Quality of life in a community is determined by a bunch of different things. Probably the most basic is: "...the air we breathe."

And the more we drive locally, for instance, the fouler the local air we breathe. In turn, respiratory problems increase, cancer rates increase and on a wider scale, global warming increases.

Or to draw from the title of a recent county-wide Science Seminar talk by Bluffton 5th grade teacher Meri Skilliter: *"Ozone Good High Up, Bad Nearby."*

One way to make it not as 'bad nearby': bicycling.

Bluffton's Andy Chappell-Dick, 34, rides his 15-year-old Raleigh, with metal baskets on the back, everywhere in town. Andy estimates he's ridden more than 4,000 miles around Bluffton in the past 11 years.

A sticker on his bicycle reads: **Question Internal Combustion**.

"We forget humanity functioned just fine for centuries without the internal combustion engine," Andy told me.

Environmental considerations are at the top of Andy's list of reasons for bicycling, citing excessive air and noise pollution generated by motor vehicles.

Andy said a hidden, and actually more paradoxical, reason for not driving is it "quickens the pace of life" and often takes up more time than it saves. He said Americans have grown so accustomed to hopping in the car for the least little thing, that they now spend a tremendous amount of time merely 'en route.'

Andy also said he doesn't feel like the odd man out in Bluffton, because there is, per capita, a phenomenal number of people who bicycle, especially during the Spring, Summer and Fall.

That number drops off significantly in the cold Northwestern Ohio winters here, yet there are still several handfuls of bicyclists (way more than most northern small towns) who continue to brave the elements.

Most notable of this group is Bob Thompson, a nurse at Blanchard Valley Regional Hospital here.

Besides his frequent around town rides in the winter, Bob regularly consults with a website for "ice bikers," and does daily 17-mile training rides out into the area's frigid, wind-swept country roads with two bicycling buddies.

Often seeing me bicycling around town as well, Bob one day asked if I wanted to come along on one of these long winter rides.

I said sure, if I could draft… in a car.

Shortly after talking to Bob, I went to www.enteract.com/~icebike/. There was a picture of West Kingston, Rhode Island's ice biker Matt Newcomb sitting on his bicycle, with Nokian W106 studded tires, leaning against a sign that marked – The Geographic Center of the South Pole.

"Mother nature is not your enemy," the website proclaims.

Maybe it's just me, but these ice bikers seem to have a 'gear' most of the rest of us don't – although I have to admit I am now thinking about getting spiked bicycle tires for next winter. I didn't even *know* there were spiked bicycle tires.

Note: An even much greater percentage of Blufftonites walk. They walk to work, on errands and for exercise. (According to a 2000 Census Survey, 432 people, an absolutely amazing number of Blufftonites, walk to work.)

Also, the ladies at the First Mennonite Church here have instituted a weekly Tuesday Night Walk, with groups of two or three traversing routes all about town in early evening.

In addition, City Council member Mitch Kingsley, who is always about town walking or on bicycle himself, is exploring taking Bluffton to yet another level.

He has recently been researching material on "Walkable Communities," developed by High Springs, Florida's Dan Burden. Burden, who was recently featured in *Time Magazine* as one of the nation's top environmental visionaries, travels the country showing towns how to become much more pedestrian and bicycle friendly.

Burden promotes designs for creative, interconnected bike and walking paths. He lists strategies for developing marked bicycle corridors along streets to make cycling safer. He promotes concepts like locating senior living facilities above downtown mercantile sections to increase elderly 'walkability.' He shows towns how to obtain right-of-ways and create diagonal paths to shorten distances from residential sections to the downtown -- and much more.

Mitch added he is currently trying to promote some town dialogue about all this.

Chapter 3

Bluffton Hero

Speaking of the South Pole...

Probably the most famous former Blufftonite of late is Dr. Jerri Nielsen, a private medical practitioner and emergency room doctor, who lived in Bluffton with her family during part of the 1990s. While here, she got a divorce and decided to get away for a while.

And *boy* did she ever get away.

At the age of 46, Dr. Nielsen opted for a year's sabbatical at Amundsen-Scott South Pole Station in Antarctica – where there is total darkness and it reaches lows of 100 degrees below zero in the eight months of winter. During most of these winter months, this area of the South Pole is inaccessible to the outside world.

(Not a good place, say, for someone with "seasonal affective disorder" – which amazingly, it's been reported Dr. Nielsen had.)

Dr. Nielsen's story began to make front page news across the globe when she discovered a lump in her breast a month after the station had closed down for the winter. According to news reports, she subsequently performed a self-biopsy, her only anesthetic being ice and a local pain killer. The biopsy showed an aggressive, fast growing cancer. The heroics in this saga continued when a month later Air National Guard pilots flew an unprecedented mission into Antarctica, when it was much too early and too cold, for a plane to safely fly. Nonetheless they made it, airdropping chemotherapy drugs.

Despite beginning to administer chemotherapy to herself, Dr. Nielsen's cancer began to spread to her brain. As the world tensely watched, and while it was still way to unsafe to fly, more Air National Guard pilots attempted a perilous rescue mission. In minus 58 degree weather (the temperature at which fuel begins to gel) and zero visibility, the plane miraculously made a safe landing at the station, quickly picked up Dr. Nielsen and started her back on her journey to the states.

She subsequently had a mastectomy and chemotherapy treatments at Indiana University, and is now apparently cancer-free. Since the operation, Dr. Nielsen has written the national bestseller (the Bluffton Public Library has four copies alone) *Ice Bound*, and she has begun lecturing around the country about her ordeal.

Chapter 4

Bluffton College Moment

The Big Orange Chair

During Campaign 2000, we had been on the road campaigning for the presidency continually for a year and a half.

Prior to leaving, we had given away our furniture, thinking there was no use just letting it sit around when someone else could use it. Besides, we knew the White House probably came furnished. (How were we to know the Clintons were going to take the end tables?)

Anyway, again, we lost the election. Consequently, our Bluffton furnishings were a bit scant at first – and the novelty of sitting on milk cartons was starting to wear off for Liz.

It was about this time our neighbor Darryl Nester, who is the "Voice of Bluffton College Sports" and scavenger extraordinaire, told us with the college letting out for the Summer that particular week, there should be a few odd pieces of furniture, etc., around the campus dumpsters.

And "odd" can best describe the chair I found outside the woman's dormitory Ramseyer Hall on my first foray. Apparently this particular student had been heavy into "retro," or a great aunt, who hadn't liked this niece much, willed her the piece.

It was a bright, almost fluorescent, orange chair, with an extremely short, flared back and a exceedingly big balloon cushioned seat. It looked to be a period piece from the '50s. And all it seemed to be missing was a black velvet Elvis wall hanging.

I was actually pretty sure Liz would rather go with the gray milk cartons still, but I put the chair in my bicycle trailer anyway.

Actually it was balanced in a rather askew fashion, atop a small, bright purple plastic chest and a funky green painting of a meadow that had also been discarded. The whole thing looked kind of like a bad Andy Warhol op-art sculpture.

And believe me, it didn't go long without being noticed.

As I passed through Ramseyer parking lot, carefully walking the bike, I noticed a rather large group of parents and students standing in a circle, holding hands. The students were seniors just about to go their separate ways in the world, and they had paused in this moment, with their parents, to pray.

However, in the moment between their hands clasping, and the first prayer being voiced, I strolled by – and all heads turned.

I couldn't resist.

Just a few steps past now, I stopped, turned toward the group who were still quite noticeably staring, and in my best (which isn't very good) refined English accent, said:

"We've decided to decorate in 'Early University' this year."

When the laughter stopped, they asked me if I wanted to join them in prayer. I said sure.

And as they emotionally asked God to be with them as they left each other for the next phase of their lives, I silently prayed Liz wouldn't 'leave' me when I brought the chair back.

Note: Today at our church, St. Mary's Catholic in Bluffton, Fr. Dennis Hardigan, in discussing the many faces of God, said Voltaire ("...or someone like him.")

wrote: "God is (at times) like a comedian playing to an audience that's afraid to laugh."

Laughter, or not, I have to believe God is using some of the episodes of my life -- for a lot of His punch lines.

Bluffton Comic:

Speaking of comedians...

One of the first woman comedians to make it in the national spotlight, actually went to school right here for a time. Born in Lima, Ohio, on July 17, 1917, Phyllis Diller went to Bluffton College from 1935 to 1937. During that time, she apparently acquired enough material (Bluffton is also said to be the "funniest town" in America) to go on to national entertainment prominence with her numerous TV, radio and movie appearances.

Ms. Diller received, among many awards, the "Best TV Comedian" award; and, "Star of the Year" award from the National Association of Theatre Owners. It is rumored, although no one has been able to substantiate this, that Phyllis's fictitious, couch-potato husband "Fang," who she refers to often in her performances, is actually a composite from her observations of a group of guys who once lived on Kibler Street here.

On October 25, 1984, she came back to her hometown for a Civic Center opening.

During a press conference, she recalled her time at Bluffton College and praised the education she got there. Later while being questioned about the "news of the day," Ms. Diller was asked her opinion of the country's first big city (Chicago) woman mayor, Geraldine Ferraro.

Ms. Diller let out her characteristic trademark laugh and said: "I thought it was a car." (Shortly after, it is was reported BC allocated a lot more money for their Political Science Department.)

Always a flamboyant dresser, and that's an under-statement, the *Bluffton News* reported this evening Ms. Diller was wearing: "a dark pink top, a bright pink skirt, light lavender hose and pink shoes. A boa of bright cloth strips adorned her neck along with a rhinestone necklace and a strand of ruby-red beads."

Now *that's* the outfit that would work with our orange chair.

Chapter 5

Et Cetera Shop

Speaking of the orange chair…

In the orange chair essay, when I wrote that Darryl Nester is a "scavenger extraordinaire," I meant it in the best sense of that phrase. In fact, he has turned what I too am finding to be a modern expression of an inbred 'hunter/gatherer' instinct into a ministry, of sorts.

Darryl, who is also a math professor at Bluffton College, knows when students are readying to move on to the "next phase of their lives," or for that matter, are just heading home for the summer, they have a tendency to leave behind (i.e. throw out) some of the stuff from the "last phase of their lives."

For instance, I found enough half containers of tooth paste, after shave and shampoo alone, that it should last our family the next five years.

Anyway, to head off some of the used clothes pitching on campus each spring, Darryl posts notices and leaves boxes in the dorm hallways to get donations for the Et Cetera Shop, a Mennonite thrift store outreach in downtown Bluffton.

Then the last week of classes, Darryl can be seen with his bicycle trailer continually ferrying loads to the shop. There, volunteers will sort, wash, iron and put Darryl's, and other town donors', items out where they sell for a fraction of what they're worth. (And actually, the store is done with such taste, and care, it's hard to tell it's a thrift store at first glance.)

The Et Cetera Shop tremendously benefits the area's lower income residents (and low-budget presidential candidates), with much of the profits going to benefit even more low-income, *extremely* low-income, people in the Third World.

Et Cetera Shop manager Missy Schrock told me she has 140 volunteers, a phenomenal number for the size of the town. What's more, some of the volunteers add to the store's profit through their own special ministries.

Royce Engle, for example, recycles used wax into some of the most beautiful candles for the store. And he definitely goes the "extra mile" for his customers.

About a month before Christmas, I asked Royce if he had any pine-scented candles. (My wife Liz is from New Zealand, and the scent of pine is a Christmas tradition there.)

Royce said no he didn't have any pine candles.

A couple weeks later, I got a call. Royce had ordered some pine-scented candle additive, or whatever you call it, from California -- and there was a candle waiting for Liz at the Et Cetera Shop.

Show me another thrift store in America, or any store for that matter, that would go to that length? *What am I tellin' ya about Bluffton, huh!*

Note: The Et Cetera Shop is the oldest Mennonite thrift store in the country, soon to celebrate its 30th year.

"Little hammer"

Speaking of Royce Engle…

Royce doesn't just do candles. He is also the founder of an extremely creative Mental Health Ministry at First Mennonite Church. It includes a weekly support group, provides a good deal of mental health literature and offers seminar series on any number of related topics.

In a recent mental health series at First Mennonite, John Kampen said society, as well as the church, can sometimes turn a deaf ear to mental health problems.

John read from the book *Circle of Caring*:

"Everything is peaceful and quiet, and only mute statistics protest: so many people gone out of their minds..."

John's wife, therapist Carol Lehman then explained 'going out of one's mind' is relative, and can, to one degree, or another, include such things as schizophrenia, bi-polar disorder, addictions... The Mental Health Ministry asked Mrs. Lehman to talk so congregation members could better understand the dynamics of these problems – so they could better help.

"Behind the door of every contented, happy man there ought to be someone standing with a little hammer continually reminding him with a knock that there are unhappy people," John Kampen also read from *Circle of Caring*.

And by the nature of what I've seen at First Mennonite, most congregation members, for the sake of the gospel, are quite willing to reside with this person with the "little hammer."

Character builder:

At First Mennonite's Mental Health seminar, therapist Carol Lehman also said for good self-esteem and strength of character, it is important youth have a consistent, nurturing environment growing up. This includes quality parental influence, positive school influence...

And to that end, Bluffton Elementary School has developed what has to be one of the most creative character enhancers in the country.

Each week the school has a "Word of the Week." This is not so much to enhance the child's vocabulary, as it is to enhance the child's character.

A word like "courage" is picked. Teachers then determine which children in their class best exemplify that word.

The names are then put in a hat and several are drawn. The winners get a blue and silver pencil with "Principal's Award" stamped on it.

Cindy Basinger's son Aaron has been nominated four times in the last year. The attributes: enthusiastic, determined, polite and 'Martin Luther King Jr.'

The *Bluffton News* regularly reports on "Word of the Week" nominees and Cindy keeps a box with all Aaron's clippings.

"Sometimes (with youth) the negative gets focused on, but not the positive," said Cindy. "This not only focuses on the positive, but gives children even more of an incentive to build their character."

Toward the end of the interview, I told Cindy to tell Aaron after being dubbed "enthusiastic, determined, polite and 'Martin Luther King Jr.,'" the next time he wins – he ought to hold out for a pen, or something.

I probably should be working on my character, huh?

Note: Speaking of Martin Luther King Jr… Bluffton third graders in Beth Raeburn's class were recently asked to write brief essays with Dr. King's *"I have a dream…"* speech as the theme. An excerpt from Beth Hieronimus's essay read: "I have a dream… I don't think we should have any more wars. All the wars scare children. I would ask the President to make a speech about peace, or the mayor of Bluffton."

Chapter 6

Common Grounds

Just a couple stores down from the Et Cetera Shop is the *Common Grounds Coffee House.* It was opened in 1997 by Pete and Kim Suter.

Over a cup of French Vanilla blend coffee, Pete told me the history.

Prior to '97, Bluffton didn't have a coffee shop, per se.

Pete and Kim, both students at Bluffton College, had been working evenings at the town's Shannon Movie Theatre, and a continual refrain of people from out of town after the flick was: "Is there a coffee shop around?"

Pete, who is now a professor of finance at BC, said he and his wife made a go of the coffee shop for three years, but 'finances' were indicating the couple was just breaking even.

They decided to close it. One problem: their friends, many of whom were also coffee shop patrons, said they wouldn't let them close it. *Again, what am I tellin' ya about Bluffton? Is this a different kind of town, or what?*

In a rather savvy, and quite unusual, business move, these patrons formed a board, established an S-Corporation and sold 100 Common Grounds shares at $1,500 a share.

Some 62 towns people came forward to buy

shares and Pete and Kim were designated to continue operating the shop.

Shortly after, a building was bought. They had been
renting at another location. Then an elaborate, and I
mean *elaborate* (hardwood floors, old fashion interior
brick façade, multi-track lighting, the whole thing...)
renovation was done.

In fact, the space morphed into the type of coffee
shop you are more apt to see in the Soho District of New
York, as opposed to a small town in the rural Midwest.

A lot of the renovation work was done by volunteers. Other volunteers, in turn, helped the regular staff
in the early phase of the shop being opened.

And by the end of the first year at the new location,
Common Grounds sales were up 45%.

Despite the shop starting to turn a profit, Pete said:
"People didn't really invest in this because they thought
they might retire early. They did it because they thought
it would be good for the town."

And more than just a good cup of French Roast
and a genial atmosphere, the esprit de corps generated by people pitching in like this for a 'common
cause,' can only enhance the quality of community in
general in a town.

And it certainly has here.

Chapter 7

Community

Speaking of community...

Another thing that adds to quality of life in a community is, well, community. That is, the frequency, quality and depth of our human interactions.

For some, particularly in this modern age, life is often "pseudo-community."

Author M. Scott Peck, who wrote a book on community building titled *A Different Drum,* describes pseudo-community as a superficial state where people, for instance, meet once a week at church on Sundays and exchange a few pleasantries, or merely wave to neighbors while out cutting the grass, or occasionally catch up for a few moments at a chance meeting in aisle 5 of K-Mart...

Also, with the evolution of 'Western individualism,' people often live now, more or less, self-contained. They spend countless hours behind closed doors in "virtual," one-dimensional relationships with TV characters, computers. They own all the stuff they need.

There's little interdependence anymore. And as a result, there's little deep, true community – which can enhance one's quality of life exponentially.

However in Bluffton, there is quite an intentional effort to create true community, starting at 123 Spring Street.

For the past eight years, Andy (the bicycle guy) and Wendy Chappell-Dick, his wife, have hosted a community potluck in their home, "…everyone welcome!"

Our family attended our first potluck there one of the first Thursday evenings we were in Bluffton, and I was absolutely taken (read: *blown away*) with the palpable sense of community – not to mention, Rebecca Kreider's seven layer bean dip was to die for.

While kids romped about out back working on their own community building in the Chappell-Dick's split-level tree house with a spiral stair case (By far, the *best* tree house we've seen in the country!); inside, adults discussed family, politics, spirituality... in such a deep way, you could tell they had quite a history with each other.

Through this regular forum, they'd been intentionally building relationships.

And while a touchstone each week, the relationships stretched far beyond the Thursday potlucks and rippled throughout the town.

Kitchen Co-op

One idea that came out of the potluck, and is actually the brain child of Wendy Chappell-Dick and Victoria Woods-Yee, is a "Kitchen Co-op."

A circle of families have begun bartering homemade granola, bagels, bread (some baked in a solar oven), salad dressing, yogurt, babysitting time… Each item is assigned a value in so many "Co-op coupons."

Wendy said the reason for the coupons was that, at times, direct barter might not work. That is, while someone might want a bag of homemade granola from Wendy, she might not have the need at that time for, say, some salad dressing from the person who received her granola. She may, instead, need yogurt.

Wendy added there have been several positive things

that have, so far, come out of the Kitchen Co-Op.

For one, she said it has moved those involved into practicing more "home arts," if you will. What's more, Co-op members find themselves eating healthier.

And, it has become a "nice social connection," and community enhancer, with Co-op members seeing and talking with each other more than normal because of all the "trading," Wendy added.

Lending list

To create even more community enhancement, and reverse even more of the self-contained Western individualism thing, the First Mennonite Church here has instituted a "Lending List" of items they offer to share freely with each other.

The items are categorized.

Under Grounds/Gardening, for instance, are: a rototiller, lawn mowers, a chainsaw, a push garden seeder.

Under Kitchen/Food Service category are: blenders, dehydrators, ice chests, canning equipment, bread machines... and ultra-expensive "glass napkin holders with little roses in them." (Now there's an item my wife and I might not be borrowing anytime soon. Joseph, our four-year-old, likes to throw things.)

But what we did decide to borrow was some camping equipment, including this one particular lantern.

1965 Coleman Lantern:

We were going on a weekend camping trip. Something we do once, maybe twice, a year. Instead of spending 25 bucks on a new lantern, we noticed our neighbor Bill Keeney had a lantern listed on the Lending List.

When I showed up to borrow it, he said he'd bought the lantern in 1965 "and it might not light the first time."

As Bill was pumping and lighting, and lighting and pumping, in the garage out back, we started talking about things.

Turns out, he's a retired professor of religion and philosophy from Bluffton College and has an annual Peace Lecture named in his honor.

As coincidence (or I'd like to think, serendipity) would have it, I was in the midst of writing my new monthly column for the *Lima News* on "peace-building" in the midst of president Bush's push to rejuvenate the "Star Wars" Missile Defense Program. My point in the column was that we need people to be more "offensive" about trying to promote peace. (But I needed a local example.)

As Bill was still trying to light the lantern, this thing was *old*, he told me he and a group of others had risked their lives going to Tehran in the midst of the Iran hostage crisis, during the Jimmy Carter administration, to promote peace and help free the hostages.

They met with some of the hostages, the students holding the hostages, the Shah of Iran's son. And, who knows, their efforts may well have helped shorten that crisis.

When I stopped taking notes, the lantern was finally lit.

Bill, in turn, said he'd read an article about our campaign in *Ohio Magazine* the year before. He asked how things were going now.

I said we had decided to run again and we were developing a campaign team locally. I also said with all the effort we were putting into the campaign, it was sometimes hard to stay solvent personally.

He said he needed his grass cut once a week.

I said sure.

By the time I got home, I not only had a lantern, I had a completed column, a side-job and a new friend. And, I also had the 25 bucks we'd saved, that could go to the poor, or efforts to promote peace, or...

And that's often, in total, how the Lending List *really* works.

Chapter 8

Painter's Plus Pause

Brush Strokes

While crunching numbers one night, it became clear the $30 a month I was making on the column, and Bill Keeney's weekly lawn job, was not going to, oh, stretch far enough. (We were so strapped, in fact, that we had kept the orange chair.)

Enter our neighbor across the street, Dale Way.

Dale, in his early 50s, had been the minister at Bluffton's United Methodist Church. Prior to that, as it often goes with pastors in the Methodist Church, he had been transferred six times over the past 16 years. He has a wife and three children.

In the face of the next transfer, he said no.

Since, he has grown a pony tail, reads the alternative *Utne Reader Magazine* and started a town handyman business called: ***Painter's Plus "…no job too small!"***

One night while talking to Dale at the Thursday potluck, he suggested I start a part-time painting business myself because, often, he needed help. And he could probably find other town jobs for me as well.

So there I was the next day, paint brush in hand, working with Dale on the interior of a two story house in Bluffton.

[As a preface, Dale colloquially refers to himself as the "painter dude." And now, after working with him on and off for some time (and sticking with the 'Bluffton

Best' theme some more), I have to say he is probably the *fussiest* 'painter dude,' and most skilled handyman -- in the country. And I'm not just *saying* that.]

Exhibit A:

I've painted before, not a lot, but some. And this initial day, I'd been breezing along fairly confidently for the first half hour, or so. It was then that Dale walked up to inspect, training a floor spot light on the area.

Hands backwards on hips, he slowly, and quite deliberately, looked from one angle to another. He then backed up to get a wide-angle view.

Finally, and with what I thought I detected to be a bit of a muted sigh, Dale drew close, put his arm around my shoulder and, as diplomatically as possible, said famous painters (Van Goh, Monet, Michelangelo, Picasso...) have taken great pains to *expose* their brush strokes to the world.

"With us," Dale continued, "it's just the opposite. A good house painter will take great pains to *hide* his brush stroke."

How's that for pressure the first day, huh?

Although I have to say I was relieved he didn't suggest I cut an ear off before doing the living room walls.

Chapter 9

It's Better To Give...

A consumer culture, like ours in America, will tell you quality of life is primarily about what you "get."

However, psychologists, sociologists, ministers, even some of the people up the street on East Elm here for that matter... will tell you quality of life is primarily about what you "give."

That is, a person's spiritual, emotional, and some will even contend, physical well being, is directly proportional to the degree and quality they are extending themselves to aid mankind.

Or put another way, you just seem to feel better when you're helping someone else.

In that light, part of how good a town is would hinge on how many avenues have been created to provide venues to help.

In Bluffton, there are many. And I'll start with the man whose house Dale and I were painting...

"No longer just statistics."

While I was 'hiding' my brush strokes, or rather *attempting* to hide my brush strokes that first week, I learned the house we were painting was that of former Bluffton College criminal justice professor Kay Hardesty.

Hardesty, it turns out, is one of the top educators in that field, and has been working jointly with prisons in the area to improve rehabilitation techniques and promote more help to prisoners from the public.

And he starts with his students. Professor Hardesty taught in a very "hands-on" fashion and over the years has set up liaisons for his classes to visit prisoners, help in domestic violence programs for offenders, join in drives to raise funds, clothing and food for needy prisoners and their families...

While there's "no magic pill or elixir" to inspire a prisoner's rehabilitation, professor Hardesty told me this kind of consistent caring and help from the outside may be just enough, in some cases, to turn the tide.

Bluffton College's professor Perry Bush is helping to turn a similar tide. Students in his Issues in Modern America class were recently given two options: write a full-length term paper, or do 15 hours of service work.

Junior Rachel Lapp opted for the latter. She tutored residents at the Worth Center in Lima, who were preparing to take their GED tests. The Worth Center is a residential facility for first-time, non-violent offenders trying to get their lives back on track.

"The people were no longer just a statistic (in a text book)," said Ms. Lapp. "They became real people with stories and concerns."

Many Bluffton College students participate in "service learning" projects through their classes. Some of the other projects have included: mentoring children of drug addicted parents for an inner city outreach, working in an area Soup Kitchen, helping on Habitat for Humanity projects...

Likewise, church members, and others, throughout Bluffton also collaborate on Habitat for Humanity projects as well, projects to help youth, projects to help seniors... In addition, almost all the churches in town are collaborating on a Bluffton Food Pantry project for low-income people in the area. It runs out of St. John's United Church of Christ.

Meanwhile back at Bluffton College, students in Deborah Myers Community Nutrition course collaborated, in a most creative way, on a Churches United Pantry (CUP) in Lima, Ohio.

To counteract a mindset that often has society 'just throwing white bread at the poor,' these students put together posters and brochures informing the 200 families involved with CUP about eating in line with the food pyramid, healthy snack suggestions and other ways to improve their nutrition.

This type of thing goes a long way in helping prevent sickness.

Helping make things run.

But if there is sickness (accidents, or whatever...), Blanchard Valley Health Campus in Bluffton is the place to go.

Not only do they have a quite qualified medical staff, but their volunteer program could easily be the best in the country, per capita, or rather, per patient.

Peggy Grandboise, director of Volunteer Service at the hospital, said she has 80 volunteers. A majority of volunteers are seniors, but Peggy said there is also a teenage volunteer program in the summers.

Because it's a small hospital, she continued, all the volunteers are extremely instrumental in helping make things run.

The most active volunteer at Blanchard Valley in recent years has been Margaret Carr, 76. She retired from the Triplett Corp. in Bluffton in 1990, and since has been volunteering at the hospital "most every day."

Margaret volunteers in the Emergency Room and in the Medical Records Dept. And she told me her volunteer work is driven by her spirituality, in tandem with a belief we are "meant to help others."

I interviewed Margaret in Blanchard Valley's small cafeteria, a place the kids and I are not unfamiliar with.

Muffin Madness:

The Blanchard Valley Health Center cafeteria, tucked in a corner of the hospital's lower level, is open to the public. But no one *knows* it's open to the public.

And the kids and I aren't tellin'.

That's because "Ms. Doreen" and "Ms. Diane" only make so many muffins every morning. These babies are homemade, they're hot, they're quite big, they're blueberry, apple, carrot raisin… and they're only 25 cents a piece! Shhhhh.

When's the last time you've come across a muffin, and a homemade one at that, that was just 25 cents – since, say, 1940!

What have I been tellin' ya about Bluffton, huh?

Ms. Doreen was telling us the other day that the now famous (and mentioned earlier) Dr. Jerri Neilsen used to occasionally work in the Emergency Room here, and, like everyone else on staff, would regularly stop in for a muffin.

A conundrum for the kids and I.

I mean, we couldn't understand how anyone could even move a few miles away from Ms. Doreen's and Ms. Diane's muffins (we live right around the corner, and we aren't moving, ever), much less 7,000 miles away to Antarctica.

While we're sure Dr. Neilsen had her reasons, all we could do is shake our heads.

Note: Liz doesn't accompany the kids and I on our morning trips to the hospital. She gets embarrassed, saying the only people who should go to a hospital are the sick, and their family and friends. However, despite this rather arcane attitude, even Liz won't let us back in the house these mornings if we haven't brought her back one of Ms. Doreen's and Ms. Diane's muffins. (She's partial to blueberry.)

Chapter 10

Painter's Plus Pause

minimalism **Musings**

One thing professor Kay Hardesty apparently likes is the color white. On this first painting job for me, we were painting the entire interior of the professor's rather large, old two-story home in flat white. Not Navajo white, or Velvet white, or Magnolia white... just plain ole' flat white.

Now, while I don't think they've ever actually done any psychological studies on this, a couple weeks of being surrounded by asylum-like white walls can, well, get to you.

Today, as has happened regularly ("It's not every day you get a chance to ask a presidential candidate questions," he says.), Dale asked me my position on the "National Endowment for the Arts."

I said in today's society, the line between art, and what's not, is really blurring – but any attempt needs to be honored.

"How so?" He asked.

First off, I told Dale I personally lean toward minimalism in my own tastes. And as an example, I continued that in the last couple weeks as I've been "engulfed" by these white walls, I had gotten an idea.

I said I had been inspired to go on the road with what I thought would be a first.

That is, instead of taking the pains to hide, or for that matter, expose, brush strokes in a "work," why not eliminate them altogether?

And along with that, why not go from museum to museum across the country, setting up displays of blank canvasses. Then people could walk about – creating their own mental pictures for each canvass.

Dale enjoined, if I was really a *pure* minimalist, I'd take that idea even a step beyond.

It was my turn to ask: "How so?"

"Why don't you just stay right here in Bluffton, and simply *think* the tour is happening, even advertise the dates," Dale posited. "Then people could just stay at home and *think* they were at the museum."

"*Wow*, 'existential art,'" I mused.

After thinking about it more, I added while I really liked the concept (and it would lend itself quite well to our gasoline conservation platform), I doubted in the current climate that we could get a Federal grant for it.

Of course, then again, maybe we could just *think* we got the grant.

Looking at my watch, I then told Dale it was time for a (Amaretto blend) coffee break.

"Why don't you just *think* you're on a coffee break?" Dale laughed, sort of.

Chapter 11

Global Bluffton

Unlike professor Hardesty's home, not everything in this world is all 'white,' or all 'black,' or all 'yellow'…

And many will tell you, rich quality of life (not to mention the promotion of peace in this melting pot we call America, and globally) has a lot to do with understanding other races and cultures.

To that end, Bluffton has shunned homogenization to become, perhaps (and per capita), the most diverse small town in the Heartland.

Bluffton, for instance, uses "the arts" in a number of different ways to help promote diversity.

A primary form: films.

One day while brainstorming about raising 'diversity consciousness' in Bluffton, Dale Way and Wendy Chappell-Dick hit on the idea of foreign films.

Each month on a Friday night, Dale, Wendy and their spouses would host a film at various locations (Common Grounds, the Grille Restaurant, library community room.)

Liz and I went to the showing of *The Color of Paradise*, an extremely touching story of a blind boy living in a village in southern Iraq. (We both cried, more than once.)

Afterward we ate Iraqi domas, grape leaves wrapped around meat. I would have to say a first for this "average Joe," who is primarily used to buns wrapped around a dog.

The Iraqi food this night was provided by Jeff and Julie Rayis. Jeff's father is from Iraq and goes back regularly to help his family.

We also discussed the film, at length.

Dale, who is also a community thespian, said the series of films they showed (inherent to many foreign films) were slower paced than the typical American movie, and focused more on human interaction than, say, high drama scenes.

In this, the American audience gets a better picture of the intricate workings of another culture and, said Dale, it "can't help but draw the global community closer together."

Dale also said it was uncanny, but when they were hosting the films, no matter where the setting of the film, Sweden, China, Ireland, Vietnam… someone who had traveled to the country, or was actually from there, would be at the film. And they often, most enthusiastically, would lead the informal discussion afterward

A large part of the reason there are so many people in Bluffton from different lands is the international understanding and diversity Bluffton College tries to promote.

Cross cultural experience

Bluffton College (and other Mennonite colleges across the U.S.) require students to do a "cross cultural" study.

Whether overseas travel, or a trip in the U.S., for anything from a couple weeks to a full semester, students learn about new cultures by living and working with the people of the region.

Some BC students had just returned from working with the Peace and Conflict Resolution program in Northern Ireland. Senior psychology major Beth Webster said the 15 weeks she spent in Northern Ireland was absolutely "life-changing." BC alumnus Eric George, who had gone on an earlier Northern Ireland trip, said he had been tremendously impacted by the Irish people's struggle, and determination, to gain peace.

The most recent semester, BC students have the chance to go to Central America, Israel/Palestine, Jamaica, Vietnam, Appalachian Kentucky, the inner city of Chicago...

And it's to the inner city of Chicago that Sarah and Benji Bergstrand, former residents of Bluffton, have gone for two years of volunteer work through the Mennonite Central Committee. (A concept suggested for young adults throughout the Mennonite community.)

A young married couple who last year toured with us on a campaign leg during the summer, Sarah and Benji headed to Chicago to teach at an inner city school for Hispanics and work at a neighborhood food pantry outreach.

Bringing the world home...

Lamar Nisly, who is an English professor at Bluffton College, and his wife Deborah, have stepped into 'international relations' with China in a highly intimate way as well.

China has a one-child-per-family policy that has left a lot of babies abandoned in bus stations, or they had been left to die in rice paddies, and so on...

After reading about the plight of these babies, especially baby girls who are less valued in that culture, the Nislys decided to help. They undertook a two-year adoption process, and this year they, and their two children, have welcomed little 9-month-old Annalise, from a foster home in Ningdu, to their family.

Lamar explained to me while Annalise will grow up in the American culture, he and his wife will do all they can to help the child learn about her Chinese heritage as well. Not only will this benefit Annalise, but Lamar said it will help the family as a whole grow tremendously in their understanding of the Chinese culture.

Meanwhile, Bluffton's Dan Wessner and Liz Holdeman have been learning about the culture in Vietnam. A married couple, they taught English and researched Vietnam during the 1990s.

Now both at Bluffton College, they are working with professors at An Giang University to create an English language curriculum and a virtual classroom that will connect the two countries.

Four Masters level students are currently here from Vietnam, living with host families and working on the project.

One of the host families is Bluffton's Monica and Steve Harnish and their three children. Monica said one of the reasons they decided to host a Vietnamese student is it was their family's way of trying to help build peace. That is, in the aftermath of the carnage and scars the Vietnam War left, Monica said the family sees this as an attempt at "healing."

What's more, in their own personal quest for "diversity," Monica said the family was also quite excited to have the opportunity to learn more about the Vietnamese culture.

While in Vietnam, Liz Holdeman and Dan Wessner adopted two Vietnamese children. And as a result, the children of Bluffton are benefiting as well.

Dan and Liz recently spoke about Vietnamese culture at their son Alex's Bluffton Elementary School class. After the presentation, students were asked reasons they might want to live in Vietnam. The *Bluffton News* reported second grader Cody Shank said: "I would like to live in Vietnam because we would eat a lot of rice. I like rice."

Note: Liz Holdeman is also the director of Bluffton College's Lion & Lamb Peace Center, which has taken the Bluffton foreign films baton and increased the showings to a movie every two weeks at their location in Riley Court on campus. And besides the adult film, a children's film is also now shown in an adjacent room.

What's more, every Friday at noon, the Peace Center hosts what they call a "Noodle Lunch" featuring, not a rice dish (sorry Cody), but rather a noodle dish from a different area of the world in order to "…acknowledge the variety of cultures represented on campus."

In upcoming months there will be noodle dishes from: Nigeria, Korea, India, Japan, Ohio…

While the poster didn't say what the Ohio noodle dish is, I can tell you my discerning, "average Joe" Midwestern palate will be quite disappointed if it's not: macaroni and cheese.

Chapter 12

Restaurant Hopping, Bluffton Style

Speaking of food…

In small town community-building, restaurants are often the main places the "stuff of life" gets shared between town-folk.

And Bluffton has, hands down, the best group of restaurants in the country.

As an example, there is the East of Chicago Pizza Co. that most definitely lives up to its name. On checking the map, I found the restaurant is indeed east of Chicago.

Then there's the quintessential small town The Grille Restaurant, which has the most longevity in Bluffton.

A lot of town, and national, politics get worked out, or at least talked about a lot, right here over morning coffee – in the shadow of a great Ralph Goings poster of a small town diner.

And while the Goings piece is absolutely striking, the best artwork in The Grille is found, well, in the Men's restroom. On the wall there, is a priceless (ok, it's a 'priceless print') Ansel Adams photograph titled: *Driftwood* from his "Mural Project 1941-42."

(Sorry ladies, I don't know. My wife wouldn't let me go in there.)

The Grille Restaurant was established circa the 1950s and has seen a lot of changes (not to mention the walls have heard *a lot* of political opinions), as it's moved forward through the decades.

Conversely, a restaurant on the other end of Main Street, which was established just a couple years ago, wants to take people back to the '50s.

A theme spot called the '50s Place, the motif is done so well, it's like actually walking into a '50s Museum.

It's got a James Dean mural, old Life Magazine covers, period roller skates, boxing gloves, wooden tennis racquets, hoola-hoops... hang from the walls and are set off by black & white checkered floors and shiny red booths.

Waitresses wear poodle skirts and the juke box plays Elvis, Frankie Valley and the like.

And, as you walk in, you are greeted by the famous (at least famous in these kind of restaurants) "Rosie's Diner" poster, with '50s era cars parked out front, tail lights actually flashing.

Out front of the '50s Place, are parking spots for Thunder Birds, Studebakers and old Cadillacs with fins and fuzzy dice. (Spots that are actually filled with these, and other vintage-type vehicles from several states, every 4th weekend in June for Bluff-ton's Annual Festival of Wheels.)

If you hopped into one of those cars and 'cruised the strip' north, to use the vernacular of the '50s, you'd come across Bluffton's downtown attempt at international cuisine. Bethel's Chinese Restaurant.

The menu features such exotic items as: Vegetable Fu Yun , Crab Rangu (with a side of bamboo shoots)... Or, if you're feeling a little less 'far eastern' on a particular visit, there's always the old, and rather unique, staple: "Chinese barbeque."

Let's remember, it is the Midwest.

And it's a big Midwest burger ("...we grind our own beef"), that's the specialty at the Pirate's Cove Family Restaurant back up the strip, around the corner and down the hill on College Ave. (A swashbuckling "pirate" is the high school mascot.)

With a panoramic view of the Bluffton High School football stadium and the Riley Creek (someone actually has to be positioned behind the goal posts on extra-point kicks so the ball doesn't go in the creek), Pirate's Cove has, perhaps, the best "understated" Christmas display in town.

In front of the parking lot is a life-size, or rather 'ice-size,' lighted snowman (oops, sorry… political faux pas: "snowperson"), with a movable arm. The arm, moving in constant slow motion (the kids stood there *forever*), continually tips the snowperson's top hat.

Christmas coming to you on your FM dial…

Perhaps the most "over-stated" Christmas display(s) in Bluffton, or in the country for that matter, can be found on Sunset Street.

Three separate front lawns there, a few houses apart, are decked out with myriads of Christmas figures – one animals, another has a nativity scene, and another depicts the story of the Good Samaritan.

While not exceptionally unusual on their own, what is highly unusual is the displays are "interactive." That is, each is equipped with a little mini 5-watt radio transmitter and those pulling up in a vehicle are instructed to turn their radios to a specific spot on their FM dial.

As the music, or narrative, starts, the figures move their arms, ring bells, light up… in synch.

And who's behind this Bluffton creative Christmas collection?

Who else: three retired engineers with apparently a *whole* lot of time on their hands.

Chapter 13

Blaze of Lights

Speaking of Christmas...

While Bluffton has a number of well known annual events, the one it is probably most known for is the annual Christmas-time "Blaze of Lights," which is always the first Saturday immediately after Thanksgiving.

People come from all over Northwest Ohio (and it's reported one year someone even came from Des Moines) for the winter extravaganza.

In the last few years, Dale Way has taken over as Blaze of Lights director. And in this endeavor, I can tell you, he goes to great lengths to "expose his brush strokes."

And broad brush ones they are, starting with the lights.

Some 10,000 lights are strung, a majority on the Presbyterian Church lawn downtown. They are strung by Dale and a group of other volunteers.

Also, since Dale has taken over, among a number of new wrinkles, the Blaze of Lights Parade now includes the high school marching band, three majorette baton groups, a Life Flight Helicopter fly-by and invitations to local and state "dignitaries."

Last year, among those dignitaries invited were city council members, local county commission, Ohio Governor Bob Taft... and it was either going to be George W., or, well, me.

Since the "average Joe" mobile, rimmed with Old Navy stars and stripes and sporting a bright red and green wreath bunjied to the grill, seemed so much more colorful than those what can be drab, old black presidential limos – Dale decided on us.

So there we were on parade night lined up just behind the Bluffton Custom Golf Graphics float, which included a green sign of a big guy swinging a club.

This was our new campaign driver Mark Schumaker's first night behind the wheel. Mark used to be a monk at the Genessee Monastery in New York. And he was going to need every ounce of spirituality he'd developed there for this particular night.

As if on cue, as Mark and the long line of other vehicles started to move forward, it began to snow, hard. And roads that were wet from an earlier day rain, started to turn to ice.

Horses trotted carefully, pulling smartly lighted carriages. Other floats inched carefully along the slippery road, as spectators cheered and waved.

Meanwhile, the "average Joe" mobile had its idle turned up a little too high for this particular road condition, it's tires were a little too bald and the brakes weren't holding all that well either.

So as Liz and I walked on either side of the van shaking hands and passing out buttons, unbeknownst to us, Mark was inside imploring St. Christopher (patron saint of travelers) to ask God to help him not run over the big golfer up front.

To make matters worse, Joseph, who, for age five now, had developed quite a fastball, was not so much throwing jaw breakers to members of the crowd, as he was trying to bean them.

And the peril continued, with Santa perched atop a ladder on the town fire truck, abruptly stopping his waving and ho, ho, hoing, as he narrowly missed being 'beaned' by the traffic light at College Ave. and Main.

After the parade, everyone gathered at a stage set up on Main St. to hear Dave Baumgartner, director of the local hit Christmas play "Amahl," recite a stirring rendition of *The Christmas Story*, snow still magically falling.

Then the countdown to the lights began.

At "ONE!" someone flipped the switch, and: nothing.

Apparently one of Joseph's jaw breakers had knocked out a transformer.

Some frantic rewiring ensued. Then there was another countdown.

"...THREE, TWO, ONE!" and all 10,000 lights flashed on at once to the customary, but never mundane, "Ohhhhhhh..."

I was standing next to Dale at that moment, and a tear came to his eyes – which promptly turned to ice, as the night was growing considerably colder.

And awful cold they looked, as the Bluffton High School Show Choir then mounted the stage in nothing more than their sweater costumes.

The kids performed two high energy numbers: the '50s sounding *Shim, Sham, Shimmy*"; and, from the movie "Pearl Harbor," the song: *There You'll Be*. Both had nothing whatsoever to do with Christmas. But the crowd loved it nevertheless.

Afterward, we too were 'shimmying,' er rather 'shivering,' and took our kids to Common Grounds for some hot chocolate.

The next day, while George W. was off doing something inane like trying to balance the Federal budget, Dale and I were following the parade route, shovels in hand, looking for horse droppings.

"This is when you really know who's in charge," Dale laughed.

Meanwhile, I was taking solace, although not much, in knowing former president Harry Truman had gotten his start shoveling the same stuff on his farm in Missouri.

Note: As part of the Blaze of Lights festivities, the Bluffton Area Chamber of Commerce sponsors buggy rides through town to view house decorations for three weeks prior to Christmas. Ride coordinator Ron Wise said they had more than 700 people take these rides this year. The Blaze of Lights also features a Christmas tree decorating contest, with some 30 businesses and civic organizations participating. And Bluffton's Vetters Lumber donated a handmade, children's play house, which was raffled off.

Chapter 14

Speaking Out, Bluffton Style

Downtown Bluffton anti-death penalty vigil being filmed by a local
TV station. At the time of the demonstration it was: 2 degrees.
(photo by Joe Schriner)

A quality of life factor, especially in a democracy like
ours, is how much a town provides a general environment
(and physical venues) for a diversity of opinion.

It is part of the essence of our civic responsibility.

In Bluffton, the physical venue for protest, the
venue to speak out in general, is the sidewalk around

a couple benches on the corner of Cherry and Main streets in the heart of the downtown. (It's the closest Bluffton has to a "square.")

And usually not a month goes by, that a group isn't out there with signs, or whatever, making a statement of some sort.

For instance, since we've been in Bluffton, Ohio has reinstated the death penalty.

Each time there's been an execution, people have been on this downtown corner with candles, signs, prayers and thoughts.

Bluffton's Bill Trollinger, who is a professor at Dayton University, said he had some thoughts at one of the death watch vigils.

While living in Missouri, Trollinger said he had become friends with Sam McDonald through a death row correspondence program. This started in 1984. They wrote, talked by phone and Trollinger visited Sam in prison.

They conversed about family, about football... and about Sam's past.

Sam had grown up black and poor in the inner city of St. Louis. He later went to Vietnam, not for the rice, but to risk his life for his country during the Vietnam War.

While there, he got a number of medals for courage, post traumatic stress disorder from the fighting and a drug habit to cope. The drug habit followed him.

On heroin one night back in the States, Sam killed an off duty police officer during a robbery to support his habit.

His appeals ran out at midnight Sept. 24, 1997 when he was executed by lethal injection.

Bill Trollinger told me this night at the vigil in Bluffton that he will keep speaking out until the laws change.

[The Bluffton Public Library, trying to be in step with some of these issues, also promotes regular book readings and discussions. The most recent was on the book: *Dead Man Walking*, which is about a Louisiana death row inmate and a Roman Catholic nun who desperately tries to help.]

War &/or Peace

Another issue people in Bluffton, particularly the Mennonites, are quite vocal about is: peace. (Mennonites believe in non-violence.)

Of late, with the possible pending war in Iraq, some Blufftonites have regularly been on the corner of Main and Cherry singing peace spirituals, praying, chanting, holding signs…

At one of the area demonstrations, Robert Sielschott was protesting *for* the war, claiming Iraqi leader Saddam Hussein was too evil to allow to stay in power.

He respectfully acknowledged the peace protestors 1st Amendment rights ("Actually, peace protestors are some of the nicest people," Sielschott told one of the news crews.), but he had a different opinion.

He told me Thomas Jefferson was quoted as saying in a democracy all these different opinions must be aired, and in that, hopefully, the one that is best, will rise to the top.

Several years earlier, a group of people in Bluffton decided allied bombing of Kosovo was not the "best" idea. Besides the street corner peace protests, Wendy Chapell-Dick and Dale Way procured a pop-up camper trailer, decorated it with Serbian children "art for peace," and moved it around town each week. They then established computer links to news agencies and human rights groups inside Kosovo.

And as the news of the "actual" toll (as opposed to some mainstream media reports) to the citizens of Kosovo came in, Dale and Wendy got the information to their fellow citizens here, who in turn, got the message out further.

Wendy said every afternoon there was a prayer vigil at the trailer as well.

Note: One of the people who saw this bombing in Yugoslavia first-hand is Indira Sultanic, now a first year student at Bluffton College. She said she was eight-years-old when the war began, 13 when it ended.

She said the war left a tremendous amount of emotional scars, a divided country and poverty, a lot of poverty. And little hope.

However, thanks to Bluffton College professor Jim Satterwhite, Indira was offered hope through a most serendipitous meeting. Satterwhite, who was in Bosnia to teach for a semester at a Franciscan Seminary, had stopped to see a friend who was teaching at a local high school. While waiting for him, Satterwhite met Indira.

Indira shared it was her hope to someday come to America to study.

Satterwhite told me the youth seemed quite sincere and motivated. When Satterwhite returned to America, he lobbied for her at BC.

BC gave Indira a scholarship.

I had met Indira at a neighborhood Christmas potluck.

Speaking of Christmas, again…

Another rather elaborate Christmas display can be found in front of Bluffton's Hair Emporium on South Main St. every year. Absolutely unique-looking, lighted snow flakes hang from the trees, a gaggle of Christmas figures adorn the lawn, and the center of attraction is also a 'gag,' or sorts, with a hair dresser in an elf suit cutting Santa's hair. The sign beside them reads: 'Tease the season…

Get it?

What am I tellin' ya about Bluffton being the

funniest town, huh!

Among the other characters in front of the Hair Emporium is a squirrel, decked out in Christmas attire, fishing in a fountain.

From what I hear, he's apparently fishing in the wrong place

Chapter 15

Bluffton Fishing Derby

"Big Roger"

Speaking of fishing…

While on the map, Bluffton might look "land locked," it, in fact, has two rather pleasant lakes: The National and The Buckeye.

What's more, The Buckeye Lake, which is located on the north end of town, has a wonderful park (pavilion, playground, basketball courts…).

An old converted quarry, The Buckeye is also home to Bluffton's Annual Trout Derby every first Saturday in May.

On this day, the normally placid lake is a frenzy with local anglers from Bluffton's Sportsman's Club who descend with small skiffs, an arsenal of rods, every lure imaginable and, of course, each person's favorite fishing hat (ya gotta have the favorite fishing hat) – to catch the "Big One."

Former Bluffton Mayor Roger Edwards explained in mid-March, a whopping 2,000 lbs. of trout are released into the acre and a half lake. Some 250 are tagged with corresponding prizes.

Each year, one of the fish's tags bears the name of an outstanding town citizen, becoming the biggest prize of all. The lucky fisherperson (again, politically correct) who catches this fish, splits a 50/50 pot.

Roger said while over the years there have been many a comical moment at the event (they used to do the kids part in the town swimming pool, with live fish, the whole thing), he particularly recalls one that involved him, a town buddy and the 50/50 pot.

The Sportsmen's Club, it seems, had never sold $5,000 in tickets, or even come close to selling $5,000 in tickets, for the 50/50 pot. So Roger and his friend Charles Swank felt quite safe in announcing, in a rather braggadocios manner, one morning at The Grille Restaurant that if the pot did top $5,000 that particular year – they'd swim in The Buckeye the day of the event.

After a momentary pause, for effect I'm sure, Roger said to me in small town, slow measured cadence:

"Charles and I just had *no idea* how cold a quarry can still be in early May."

Incidentally, one of the years, the 'top trout,' if you will, was named "Big Roger" after the very same Roger Edwards.

The reason Roger had been so memorialized that year was for his volunteer supervision of the "Depot Project."

Nickel Plate RR had an antiquated depot building here they were going to raze, or move, but first offered it to Bluffton, free. The stipulation: It had to be removed from the property it was on within 30 days.

Roger quickly rounded up a crew of volunteers, got some heavy moving equipment, hoisted the building and moved it a couple miles – placing it at the west end of The Buckeye Lake where it was presented to the Sportsmen's Club.

The volunteer crew then sand blasted and painted (Roger owns the paint store in town) the outside of the depot.

Inside, Roger (who also has a handyman flooring business) pulled the rotting planks and talked the high school into donating their old-hardwood gymnasium floor, which was just being replaced that year.

The floor was stripped, redone and an authentic railroad crossing sign was put out front.

And besides Sportsmen Club functions, the depot is also available to the public (for a nominal fee) for birthday parties, wedding receptions, and the like.

Chapter 16

'Buy Bluffton'

"Buy Bluffton" some Chamber of Commerce literature reads.

And people are.

In fact, Blufftonites have been so conscientious about buying locally that most small businesses here are thriving. However that, by no means, is a consistent trend across-the-board these days in small town America.

As Wal-Marts, K-Marts and other "super stores" move to an area, small town businesses die, often in droves.

And as that happens, a vital part of community-building dies.

Small town downtowns are configured for a square dance, if you will.

That is, say, a typical Saturday morning trip to town would have 'Betty Bluffton' walk into the pharmacy where she "grabbed her partner," talking with Marge while waiting for a prescription, then she would "sashay" (all innocent enough) with Chuck for a brief conversation on her way to Providence House on Vine St. for a decorative basket, then she would "change your partner (again)" while sitting to share a cup of Common Grounds Amaretto coffee at an outside bench with Elaine, and finally it would be "allemande left" (I looked that up. Who am I kidding, I looked them all up.) down to the small local market, Dave's -- to "docey-doe" and "promenade" with everyone else in town.

In this, hokey metaphor and all, the quality and depth of community grows exponentially.

The alternative: a frenetic, and just as antiseptic, dance (think punk rock gyrations) through a maze of super store aisles with people from a seven town area, most of whom you don't know.

In this, the quality and depth of small town community diminishes exponentially. (But hey, a small price to pay to get those t-shirts so cheap, huh?)

Another reason to shop locally? It's a boon to town finances in a myriad of ways.

The 'Bluffton buck' stops here

As an experiment, I traced some 'Bluffton Bucks,' if you will, through town.

First, I followed handyman Dale Way to the locally owned True Value Hardware Store on Main Street here. There he purchased a lime green six-in-one screw driver, to go with his lime green cutter-knife -- and his lime green tennis shoe laces. *And I'm not kidding!*

Anyway, store own Jeff Kantner, who is, by far, the most helpful hardware guy in the whole country, told me these new six-in-one screw drivers are the latest hardware rage. (Apparently these things can screw stuff in you don't even *want* screwed in.)

The screw driver costs about six bucks at True Value here.

A percentage of the six bucks will then go toward the purchase of some town Little League uniforms from the Sports Warehouse next door. As he can, Jeff likes to support the town youth.

The rest of the six bucks will go to, say, a hardware store business account at Bank One in Bluffton.

On a trip to Bank One next, the first thing I noticed in the lobby was a big display board featuring pictures and a write up on Jerry Marshall's Barber Shop in Bluffton. In recent months, the bank has featured a series of local businesses: Dave's Market, Little Red Barn Flower Shop, Riley Creek Mercantile, Deer Creek Antique Mall...

The display on Jerry's Barber Shop noted Jerry had been in business in his Main Street location since 1958. What the display didn't note is Jerry is apparently the most ardent 'Buckeye Barber' in Ohio, maybe the country. He has both a sign saying: *Ohio State Fan Parking Only* in his window and a maize and blue University of Michigan welcome mat – to wipe your feet on.

(It is said the night Ohio State won the National Championship in football this year, to celebrate Jerry left his barber poll running all night out front. *Do people in Bluffton know how to whoop it up, or what!*)

Shark cartilage

The barber shop display at the bank also featured a strap for sharpening the old straight edge razors and an old-fashioned brush used to apply shaving cream.

When I asked what the 'barber lingo' term for that type of brush was, Bank One's Dave Lundgren (who'd looked like he could use a shave himself) knowledgeably replied: "It's an old-fashioned brush used to apply shaving cream."

While Bank One's assistant vice president Darlene Hollar didn't know the official barber term for the brush either, she did know that some of the deposited Bluffton Bucks for the screw driver purchase would be invested. And she told me some of the return on the investment might be used for such things as helping Bluffton's Child Development Center.

Bank One had just donated $1,500 to this cause.

Some of the investment return might also go toward

account interest that may allow 'Betty Bluffton,' who has perhaps been doing a bit too much actual square dancing of late, to purchase some shark cartilage from Bluffton's Whole Food Store to help with her arthritis.

As a result, Whole Food Market co-owner Jon Sommers may be so ecstatic he finally sold a bottle of shark cartilage pills, that he takes one of the Bluffton Bucks next door to the Common Grounds Café to celebrate with a cup of organically grown Sumatran Splendor blend, a "fair trade" coffee from Guatemala.

So not only does Common Grounds benefit, but some of that particular Bluffton Buck goes toward ending Third World poverty in Guatemala, said Common Grounds employee Rhonda Blevin.

Because Common Grounds has gotten enough Bluffton Bucks (including a number from me), it is able to help provide a good standard of living for Ms. Blevin, who, in turn, may be motivated to stop down at Bluffton's Ten Thousand Villages Store to help other people's standards of living globally – while also helping with world peace. (Ten Thousand Villages is another Mennonite outreach.)

At Ten Thousand Villages, Ms. Blevin may buy, for instance, an olive wood cross. Store manager Missy Schrock told me this particular cross comes from the West Bank. And the purchase will help an artisan's family there, that perhaps, may also be actively advocating for peace on the front lines in that troubled Middle Eastern region.

And Ms. Blevin's purchase will help them keep going another day, another month.

What's more, who knows, if others in Bluffton see Ms. Blevin's new cross, they too, may start taking some of their Bluffton Bucks down to Ten Thousand Villages, which, in turn, might motivate Mrs. Schrock to go across the street to the *Ye Old Haus of Cards* for some "Thank You" stationary.

On my last Bluffton downtown stop, I asked *Haus of Cards's* Barb Mikesells why she thought it was important for Blufftonites to spend their Bluffton Bucks here.

She simply replied:

"To keep business in town – so we have a town."

Enough said.

Meat Market:

Another piece of 'Ohiocana,' that is alive and well in Bluffton is the town meat market. Town & Country Meats offers a wide variety of meat, Amish cheeses, and so on.

The meat market, which is one of the more lively spots in town, has a good deal of regular activity and lively banter. In fact, on a really busy Saturday morning, it's atmosphere most reminds me of the famous Seattle fish market, where workers there banter with the crowd as fish fly everywhere.

Town & Country's Michael (just call me "Bud") Bailey, however, has shied from similarly tossing sides of beef, citing FDA regulations against "beef tossing."

Bluffton Slaw Cutter Co.:

Bluffton also boasts a practically one of a kind company that makes a one of a kind product: the Bluffton Slaw Cutter. The blades of this product, patented in 1915, are "hammered stamped" in an old world process, said Bluffton Slaw Cutter Co. president Tim King. King said the slaw cutter makes: cole slaw, sauerkraut and some of the best darn homemade potato chips. The Bluffton Slaw Cutter was recently featured in *Reminisce Magazine* and King said this little factory in Bluffton gets orders from all over the country. In the last

week, King said he'd gotten orders from Texas and
Missouri. The small factory is open for informal
tours practically anytime.

Vision Task Force

Jeff Boehr, owner of Bluffton's Boehr Print
Shop, is on the Vision Task Force for the renovation
of the downtown here.

While already quite eye catching, over a multi-
phase, three year process, downtown sidewalks will
be improved, more outdoor plants will be added and
owners will be encouraged to revamp their store-
fronts with historic themes in line with how the
facades looked in the "old days."

Jeff also said historic looking street lights are being
discussed, with a modern twist.

That is, Jeff said there is a more efficient, new type
of light bulb that trains the light only down at the street
or sidewalk, as opposed to the old ones that unnecessar-
ily disperse light to the sides, and up.

Bluffton's Ron Rich would go for that.

Chapter 17

An 'Unlightened' America

I had gotten a job painting Ron Rich's porch on Spring St.

He is a former dean and professor of science at Bluffton College. Ron also taught at Stanford University. And in his college days at the University of Chicago, one of Ron's professors was the famous scientist Enrico Fermi.

During coffee breaks (generally with Common Grounds "Big City" blend, in honor of Chicago and other large metropolitan areas), professor Rich shared some of his philosophies so our presidential platform would be a bit more informed when it came to things of science.

One area, which we hadn't given much thought to, was "light pollution."

Professor Rich said there is way too much unnecessary light in the U.S., whether too many street lights, spotlights on buildings, household lights that don't need to be on...

The professor continued this does two things: wastes valuable energy and dims our view of the stars. (He is also an extremely avid astronomer, who never, and I mean *never*, misses NPR's one-minute nightly "Star Date.")

Professor Rich continued a tremendous amount of "untrained light" (and wattage) is wasted as the light is diffused upward, or for that matter, sideways.

Professor Rich's home abuts Bluffton College, and it was this 'sideways light' into his and his wife Elaine's second-story bedroom from a nearby walkway bulb, that finally prompted a stealth mission, if you will, onto the campus late one evening.

With step ladder and a small can of black paint, professor Rich headed off to lightly touch up the sides of the offending, cylindrical light fixture – so the light merely shined down "where it should be going anyway," he said.

When I went back to my own painting, I couldn't help but think of the millions, maybe billions, of dollars we'd save every year if the light merely shined "where it should be going anyway."

I also couldn't help but think how this savings could go tremendously far in bringing the basics of electricity to a good deal of the Third World.

And, I also couldn't help but think – albeit a fleeting "average Joe" thought – that when we got to D.C., we could create a new Federal position: Secretary of Light. We'd then appoint professor Rich, step ladder and black paint in hand, to set out to enlighten, or rather 'unlighten,' America.

I think the porch paint fumes are starting to get to me.

Wood craft:

Speaking of less wattage, or lack thereof altogether, one of the more unique places in Bluffton is Andy Chappell-Dick's Woodworking Shop behind his home on Spring St. A throw back to the "old days," he does custom woodworking without electrical power. On any given day, with NPR classical music in the background, sunlight streams in on old planes, saws, chisels... hanging from the shop's walls. In the middle of the room is a Senaca Falls

Manufacturing Co., foot-pedal table saw, circa 1895. "We are so awash in mass produced woodworking, I believe there's a value in doing things slower," Andy muses.

Chapter 18

Painter's Plus Pause

Marching to a different oboist

Ron Rich and Andy Chappell-Dick aren't the only ones in Bluffton who listen to National Public Radio…

In all my traveling across the country, and in all the handyman crews I've come across in those travels, the one common denominator I've observed, or rather heard, in conjunction with the crews, is: music.

It's always on. It's always loud.

Many crews listen to rock, either oldies or the newer stuff.

Many other crews listen to country, from Johnny Cash to the more contemporary Tim McGraw.

Painter's Plus, on the other hand, is the only handyman crew I've ever come across – that listens to classical music on NPR.

Dale regularly works with Greg Mohr, a Bluffton College alumnus who graduated with a major in music.

Often, in what I've come to regard as jovial, yet on the other hand 'culturally enlightening,' moments -- amidst intense hammering, sawing and other handyman raucous -- Greg will abruptly stop, turn an ear to the radio and announce something like:

"Hey… can you guys hear the oboe in that piece?"

Only in Bluffton.

Chapter 19

'Beeutiful' Music (Not)

Speaking of music…

Bluffton College's Yoder Hall is the stage for an Artist's Series that is next to none every year. And it's all open to the public.

In addition, Bluffton also has, arguably, the best music reviewer in the land.

Example: In a recent *Bluffton News* review, Dave Baumgartner wrote of a Yoder Hall performance by the New York based vocal sextet Equal Voices:

> **"Equally adept at sweet lyric legato or pinpoint, scattered staccato, they consistently dive, dart, spin and interplay in an involved celebration of close tonal transparency and uncanny accuracy and refinement."**

Whew, huh? Whatever that meant.

And Baumgartner doesn't just blow all sunshine up the group's larynx. When he has to, he is able to pan with the best of them:

> **"I found them (Equal Voices) less successful in the arrangement of 'Down by the Riverside,' with varying degrees of self-conscious attempts to swing along, clearly articulated harmonies notwithstanding; and I felt the 'Sweet Honey**

Sucking Bees' madrigal might have profited from a more sprightly tempo..."

So there!

After the review, I have to believe the group caught the next flight back to New York to work on their "swing along" and liven up the bee song. (In my book, there's nothing worse than a bee song that isn't "sprightly.")

The following week was the Bluffton College Music Department's Winter Instrumental Concert, featuring the Community College Band and College Jazz Band.

The Jazz Band, for instance, played exceedingly 'sprightly' versions of: *Jammin' on the Railroad*; and, *Can't Help Lovin' Dat Man* -- which Dave gave two thumbs.

However, he did throw rare "unambiguous darts" at the town for not better attending this event, which was free and open to the public.

BC music professor Steve Jacoby told me the college tries to draw the public to the Yoder Hall stage consistently. They've developed a Community Chorus, Community Concert Band, which rehearses every Monday night during the school year.

The college also stages several performances throughout the year that feature community member vocalists and musicians.

As an example, Steve pointed to the Christmas-time performance of *Handel's Messiah*, which has been conducted every second Sunday in December – since 1897. Steve explained the longevity of this show has lent itself to as much as three generations of family members participating in this, sometimes all on the same stage.

In fact, *Handel's Messiah* has such a deep history in the town that Bluffton's Earl Lehman felt compelled to capture some of the stories in his book: *A*

History of the Choral Society (One Hundredth Anniversary of Messiah by Handel).

"Tuesday Night Live..."

Just a few years back, Wendy Chappell-Dick hit on an idea to create a regular venue for local musicians. Collaborating with Pete Suter at Common Grounds, they decided on a one-hour Tuesday night gig at the café from 9 p.m. to 10.

Wendy told me she believed this would bring more local people together, while also promoting more "town music making."

One case in point was Wendy's friend Steve Walker, who was an excellent guitarist – with stage fright. After several "low intensity" stage opportunities at Common Grounds, Steve has grown more confident.

Besides Steve, other Tuesday Night Live performers have included the likes of Travis Hodosko, reggae and jazz influence; "A La Mode," acoustic rock influence; "A La *Me*," ham influence (karaoke night). Just kidding. Liz nixed it. She thought I'd lose votes.

Actually, over Vanilla Nut Decaf blend one Tuesday night when we could get a babysitter, Liz and I listened to Wendy Chappell-Dick, a quite accomplished performer in her own right, passionately sing spirituals and peace songs to an intimate crowd at Common Grounds, Joan Baez influence.

Note: Dale Way, and his wife Janet, are currently coordinating the Tuesday Night Common Ground performances, including providing, and operating, the sound system for the entertainers.

Chapter 20

'Wood' that there be art'

Bluffton also has a number of venues to support the "visual arts" as well. Probably the most frequented viewing venue, that is besides The Grille's restroom to see the Ansel Adam photograph, is the Grace Albrecht Gallery at Bluffton College.

The driving force behind the Gallery is BC art professor Gregg Luginbuhl.

The Gallery features shows by both students, and other artists. And this gallery, too, is open to the public.

I, being one of the public, recently stopped in at the Gallery to view the display: "Material & Process" by BC's Bill Millmine.

It was a showing, for the most part, of primitive, and not so primitive, stone sculpture. Also, there was one wooden sculpture I was particularly taken with called: "Harvest of the Element."

While out cutting some firewood one day, Millmine came across some oak that he felt was more suitable for art, than burning. He cut rather large pieces and fashioned them into a rough jig saw puzzle. Then he cut abstract patterns, stained them and hung them up.

He said in all this he was trying to capture the essence of cutting wood.

I was absorbed with the piece for a good 15 minutes (much longer than my usual "average Joe" attention span), recalling some of the times I had gone to cut wood. I recalled, too, how exhilarating, even primitive-feeling, the experience had been for me.

I had apparently connected with my 'inner-Neanderthal' during those times.

The viewing, serendipitously enough, would also help sway me to decide on a home we'd been looking at that had a wood stove.

Anyway, a price list indicated Millmine wanted $2,000 for this particular piece. And while, I'm sure, it's worth it; I simply couldn't justify that expenditure at this time. (Have I mentioned it's a low budget campaign?)

So I did, what I thought, was the next best thing.

I wrote Millmine a check for $10 and a note that, in part, said: "...thanks for the experience and keep on with your art." (I should be able to make the 10 bucks up in heating costs next year.)

Besides the art displays, which change every month, the Gallery hosts a reception, which is open to the public as well and allows time for the artist to explain their work.

Ketchup art

And in the vein of explaining one's art, I'd like for someone to explain to me the big ketchup bottle sculpture over at the library...

Every March the Bluffton Public Library sponsors a Youth Art Month Exhibit, with displays placed all over the library. This year there were wonderfully done pencil drawings, water color and acrylics of cityscapes, a guitarist, a rainbow, a dolphin... and this 'super-sized,' red and white, painted cardboard Heinz Ketchup bottle, which, according to a library news release "...attracts immediate attention."

And I'll second that.

It stands almost six feet tall. And from its berth atop a

book shelf, the ketchup bottle almost touches the ceiling.

In fact, Bluffton High School senior Corrie Fett's piece has such a prolific presence, I told Liz I had felt this strong compulsion to get a book, and a burger.

"Cross pollination of ideas."

Wendy Chappell-Dick, who is also the director of Bluffton's Chamber of Commerce, said she has been recently working with a collective of town artists to look for a common space (they'd initially been considering converting an old mill in town) for a Co-operative to generate and display their works. Wendy said the venue could be used in tandem with other space for musicians and others in the creative arts.

Wendy added such a place would also be a wonderful setting for a "cross-pollination of ideas."

Note: Another venue for a "cross-pollination of ideas" (I love that phrase), and some pretty darn good art (and crafts), is Bluffton's Arts & Crafts Festival. It is held every 3rd Saturday of May downtown.

Famous Bluffton artist

An artist that sometimes has a booth at the Arts & Crafts Festival, and has quite a bit of national repute as well, is Bluffton's Oscar Valasquez. Oscar grew up doing migrant work in the fields here.

He went on to art school in Cleveland, and after numerous regional and national awards, has been listed in the book: *Who's Who in American Art.*

One of the things Oscar is most noted for are his murals.

Sponsored by Bluffton College's Lion & Lamb Peace Center, Oscar went to Subotica, Serbia to paint a mural titled: *Peace Thru The Arts.*

Then he came back to America to do an absolutely striking mural of children of the world playing together, titled: *A World of Youth, Hope and Peace* – which is on display at the BC Peace Center.

In addition, Oscar's work is in stores around Bluffton and on display at the Bluffton Public Library.

And, Oscar has also turned the side of a rather large building in town into an elaborate mural of Bluffton in the "old days," complete with a trolley car that features an actual light that shines continuously.

Oops, shouldn't have said that. Ron Rich will be down there this evening with his black paint.

Bluffton Bears:

Oscar Valasquez's mural is on the side of a building that also features artists. "Teddy artists."

I'm serious, that's what they're called.

Bluffton's Groves Bears is the biggest stuffed animal emporium in Ohio, perhaps in the whole Midwest.

Why in Bluffton, a town of a mere 3,877 people (and not all of them kids)?

No one seems to know.

But it's here. *Boy*, is it here!

Stuffed dogs, cats, orangutans, zebras, horses, even a multi-colored lizard (which, frankly, you don't see much of in these parts), and the local favorite: beavers – Bluffton College team mascot.

However, what Groves Bears is most noted for is, well, bears.

They feature the work of more than 100 "teddy artists," one of the most popular being the German made Steiff bears. A store employee told me they get orders for these particular collectible bears from all over the world.

Not to mention people drive hundreds of miles to visit the shop.

Chapter 21

Free air all around!

Now for those who drive hundreds of miles to Bluffton to see the bears, or lizard, in the off chance of a vehicle break down, you're in good (albeit greasy) hands. Bluffton, 'greasy' hands down, has the best collection of service garages in the country.

And (Are you ready for this?), the air is still free at each place. *Where are you going to find a town in America with that much free air anymore, huh?*

You can confidently take your deflated tires, and other automotive woes, to Kirtland on Main, Bluffton Alignment & Tire, Lugibihl Auto, or Leiber Garage where owner Dwain Leiber has gained some of his mechanical know how working on his beloved #62 Sprint car, which he races on area tracks.

The other place to take a vehicle for repairs in Bluffton is Dotty's Garage – which, living up to its name, is actually an old converted garage out behind Thomas and Amy Dotty's home on Jefferson St.

Amy told me their son Michael is now working with his father. And she added, like fathers working with sons, she also believes small Mom & Pop businesses, like the one they have, are "the backbone of the country."

And it was the 'backbone' that Thomas Dotty would be lying on after I brought the "average Joe" mobile to his garage for a fan belt adjustment recently. (The belt was starting to squeal.)

Now, getting to the fan belt thingamabob (that's amazing, the spell check says that's actually a word) is no easy task.

Thomas slid under the engine, contorted his body as much as possible, grunted, trying to loosen something that probably hadn't been loosened since 1974, grunted some more, finally popped it loose, banging his knuckles (the grunt turned to other utterances), readjusted the thingamabob with more considerable effort, tightened the screw – and had me start it up.

No squeal.

Labor intensive elapsed time: 25 minutes.

Charge: $5.

I don't know about you, but in my book, that's even more amazing than "thingamabob" being a word!

Now, this particular service job didn't require parts. But if a job does, one of my favorite scenes in Bluffton ensues.

Thomas, who has an extraordinarily large build (stature of, say, a former defensive tackle), hops on his small, and I mean *small*, 50 cc red Honda motor scooter. He then putts (with the balance of an Olympic gymnast) up to the downtown Siferd-Hossellman Co. parts store.

Not only is this one of those priceless, signature small town scenes; but on the pollution side, it's way better for the environment than if, say, Thomas was driving a standard SUV, or 4 by 4.

Chapter 22

Bluffton 'learns to like dandelions'

Speaking of the environment...

Bluffton College graduate Bernadette Noll, a biology and education major, once said: "Everything we do affects nature, and that in turn affects us."

With that paradigm, and in that spirit, the town of Bluffton has to be one of, if not *the*, most environmentally conscious towns in the country.

For instance, besides the walking/bicycling stuff; everyone in town (except this one guy on Magnolia Ave., and you know who you are) recycles, voluntarily.

There's a curbside service, and on trash days the town becomes a sunny potpourri, if you will, of bright yellow recycling containers.

As with the efforts around recycling, many people around here also go to great pains, or actually less pains, not to put weed killers, pesticides and chemical fertilizers on their lawns because of the damage to the water table and potential carcinogenic hazard to their neighbors.

Clustered throughout town last summer, for instance, were: "This Lawn is Pesticide Free" yard signs.

The Chappell-Dicks, who had one of these signs posted in their front yard and use an engineless push mower because of pollution, also had a fairly good crop of dandelions last year. Because of the concern about yard chemicals on their two young daughters,

Sara and Hannah, the Chappell-Dicks have simply: "Learned to like dandelions."

Eco-diversity

Bluffton's Bob and JoAnn Antibus not only like dandelions, they like everything in nature. JoAnn teaches science at Bluffton High School and Bob teaches biology at Bluffton College.

(Over nightly dinner, it's rumored they talk about things most of the rest of us wouldn't even have a clue how to spell.)

JoAnn was also an exchange student to New Zealand a number of years ago, and had Liz and I over for some New Zealand slides and a tour of their rather unusual yard.

They have, in effect, turned part of the yard into a "backyard habitat."

After much research, they have planted many things indigenous to the area. The yard is filled with native trees, prairie grasses, butterfly bushes, ferns, herbs... and a medicinal "blood root," which actually looks like it's bleeding when it periodically emits its bright red sap. (I think I'd stick with the less gruesome Maple sap myself.)

Bob said having a variety of these types of trees and plants does a couple things.

One, because these native species are 'acclimatized' to the area, they are quite "low maintenance," said Bob, not needing fertilizers or pesticides. He also explained the habitat these trees and plants provide, in turn, provide natural pesticides (birds eat the insects, and so on...)

"There's an argument in ecology that diversity (there's that 'Bluffton word' again) is important," said Bob.

To take this even a bit farther than the yards, Bluffton College has preserved a rather large, species diverse Nature Preserve, which professor Antibus's biology classes, and many other local classes in Bluffton have used. It, too, is open to the public.

We regularly take our kids out "exploring" there, heading the words of a former Audubon Society instructor we met in Connecticut during one of our campaign tours:

"Youth have to fall in love with nature – before they'll want to save it," she said.

Professor Antibus continued it seems these days that many youth are falling 'out of love' with nature. He said while young children consistently demonstrate fascination with nature, as they grow they incrementally start to move farther and farther from outside environs, for more temperature controlled or sod environs.

Tree City USA

As with the Bluffton College Nature Preserve, trees very much fit into the natural motif of the town proper, because Bluffton is a Tree City USA town.

Tree City USA is a federal program. And to be a Tree City USA member the town must have: a tree board; a tree ordinance; an operating budget of $2 per person in the town; and, have some sort of Arbor Day observance.

Tree board member Jon Sommers said last Arbor Day, the Tree Board mustered a group of community volunteers to plant 500 ash trees in Bluffton's Village Park.

Sommers, who we met watering and pruning some young trees on the tree lawn in front of True Word Tabernacle downtown, said trees absorb carbon dioxide and create wind breaks in the winter, and shade in the summer, to help cut down, for instance, on energy use.

They also become an intricate part of a delicate ecosystem if found along the banks of a creek, like Bluffton's Riley Creek, which runs through the center of town.

A recent 'arbor brouhaha' has erupted in Bluffton over these trees along the Riley.

Farmers upstream, citing flooding and other problems, are calling for natural river debris, and the trees
along the bank, to be cleared to help with water flow. A
good number of farmers refer to the entirety of the river
as a "ditch," which is literally what it would look like if
the driftwood, rocks, trees… were removed.

In typical Bluffton activist fashion, the town envi-
ronmentalists have formed a coalition, spoke out
adamantly at public meetings, barraged the *Bluffton
News* with letter to the editors… and so far, the bulldoz-
ers have been staved off.

At Bluffton College's end, professor Antibus has
been put on a "Creek Committee" to monitor develop-
ments. Bob also gives public presentations on creek
ecosystems, and the like.

And there are even unconfirmed reports that if the
farmers persist, Bob is thinking about taking up 24-hour
residence in one of the trees along the Riley's banks. A
tremendous sacrifice -- because Bob is one of the town's
more avid joggers.

Chapter 23

Bluffton Globetrotter

Speaking of jogging...

I run myself, and now knowing Bob Antibus, I would be quite empathetic if he had to accede to running in place on a platform in a tree for any extended period of time.

In fact, I have developed a 'passing' camaraderie with many of the other town joggers as well. And there's a fairly high percentage of "regulars" out there.

There's hardly a day that goes by that I don't see Bluffton Schools Superintendent Steve Castle, loping along with his archetypal runner's physique that has "marathon" written all over it.

Then there's Bluffton College creative writing professor Jeff Gundy, whose short sturdy physique has "10K Race, maybe" written all over it.

Jeff, like us all, runs for health. An accomplished author, Jeff also runs to compose.

A line from one of his poems, which was recently used by Bluffton College's president Lee Snyder in her 'State of the College Address': "When I was a path, everybody thought they used me – but they all walked where I led them."

Whew... Tell me that inspiration didn't come running down some solitary stretch of country back road around here. But even as impressed as I am with all that, the jogger I most have to tip my tattered running shoes to is: Bluffton 'globe trotter' Paul Klassen.

The *Bluffton News* reported that on December 25, 2002, this retired BC social work professor completed a 24,901.55 mile jog around the world – without even leaving Ohio.

Existential jogging?

Well, no not exactly.

As a New Years resolution in 1968, Paul started running as part of a YMCA Wellness Program in Canton. He would run every day and keep a mileage journal.

Several years later, Paul moved to Bluffton, still running, still keeping track of his mileage.

Somewhere along all this, Paul thought if he could keep going, his mileage "path" could lead him around the world. So he found out how far it was.

Now, thinking the Andes, the Himalayas, and for that matter, a jog through the Pacific Ocean, might be a bit problematic; Paul stayed on Kibler, Thurman and Huber streets in Bluffton. Four miles a day, every day.

And through retirement, a pace maker and some pulled muscles (but unbelievably no serious injuries those 34 years), Paul made it, at age 78.

He crossed the figurative finish line in Wadsworth, Ohio (no slight to Bluffton, it was just that his son John and his family, threw him a Champaign breakfast that Christmas morning).

Under the Christmas tree with Paul's name on it: a globe.

Paul told me the thing he *most* developed from this phenomenal accomplishment was not strong legs, or a strong heart, but rather: a strong sense of discipline.

'Runs Like a Beaver':

When they are not running on the high-tech surface track at new Dwight Salzman Stadium, Bluffton College track & field runners can be seen running throughout town as well.

Now while I'd like to say, as I've said with certainty about almost all of Bluffton, that BC's track team is also the best in the country -- I'd have to admit, I'd be stretching it a bit there.

They win some. They lose some.

My theory on why they aren't sweeping the national meets: their mascot.

As I mentioned earlier, the Bluffton College mascot is: "the beaver."

According to sports information director Tim Stried, some 70 years ago, long-time coach and athletic director A.C. Burcky suggested using the beaver as a mascot. (With all due respect, for the life of me I can't understand why someone didn't suggest Coach Burcky have another cup of French Roast coffee on that one.) Burcky's rationale was the beaver represented the spirit of the student-athletes: "intelligent, hard working and with a determination to get the job done."

Meanwhile, it's my educated guess the *real* beavers were merely down at the Riley here not so "intelligently," but nevertheless instinctually, busily 'getting the job done' when it came to starting to disrupt the flow of the creek.

Anyway, Stried reports the first beaver insignia appeared on the track team's white shirts in 1927. And therein, I believe, lies the problem.

While over the years, the beaver insignia has changed from a rather passive looking, sort of chubby, beaver head, to a much more aggressive, toned-looking beaver head – it's still a *beaver head.*

I'm sorry, but when I think beaver, I just don't think *fleet afoot.*

And those poor BC track people, they keep trying to overcome this thing.

The most recent attempt: A number of student-athletes are now wearing t-shirts around campus, that are a take off of the contemporary John Deere ad slogan: "Runs Like a Deere."

The green shirts display BC's mascot atop a tractor with the words: "Nothing Runs Like a Beaver."

Now ok, maybe: "Nothing Runs Like a Chee-tah," or, "Nothing Runs Like a Gazelle," or even, "Nothing Runs Like a, well, a Deer..."; but, "Nothing Runs Like a Beaver?"

A raccoon runs like a beaver! An aardvark runs like a beaver! A little pudgy porcupine runs like a beaver...

Chapter 24

" Put me in coach…"

Elbert Dubenion in his Bluffton College days.
(photo courtesy of Bluffton College.)

Speaking of sports…
A Bluffton College athlete who ran like a gazelle, cheetah, deer and a rare, but awful fast beaver, all rolled

into one, was: Elbert Dubenion.

Touring a rather impressive BC Sports Hall of Fame in Founders Hall, I read that the late '50s (the years Dubenion was at BC) was "the greatest era" of BC football. Between 1956 and 1959, the football team posted a 20-0 record in the Mid-Ohio Conference – a feat that's never been repeated.

During that time, Dubenion, who was a half-back, averaged a phenomenal 9.4 yards a carry and amassed 4,734 career yards. Dubenion then went on to play flanker-back for the Buffalo Bills, catching 294 passes for 5,294 yards. (He was touted as being one of the three fastest men in the league.)

Ron Lora was a split end for BC, playing all four years with Dubenion.

Of all the spectacular plays, and there were many, Lora said he most remembers one particular Dubenion run against Hiram College.

They were playing away that day and Dubenion hadn't dressed because of an injury. BC was down at half-time and Dubenion asked then Coach Kenny Mast if he could play. The coach said ok, and Ron said Dubenion then borrowed his roommate's uniform "which was a bit ill fitting."

On Dubenion's first play in, he took the ball and raced 80 yards for a go ahead touchdown (which would prove the margin of victory). Dubenion then sat down for the rest of the game.

"It was really quite mythical," said Lora.

Although perhaps not as 'mythical,' Lora was named First Team All Ohio Conference his senior year, catching 15 passes. While not a phenomenal amount of receptions, what was phenomenal was seven of the receptions went for touchdowns – which is still a BC record… and good enough to land Lora in the BC Hall of Fame.

Ron Lora still lives in Bluffton, as does BC Hall of Famer Everett Collier, who graduated in 1975.

No. 66, Everett was a pulling guard, who received "honorable mention" as a National All American and played in the Ohio Shrine Bowl. He is now Bluffton's Postmaster, has "EC 66" on his license plate, and on a rare bad day -- Everett still appears as if he's looking for someone to block.

On his good days, Everett is also a college sports referee and a rather accomplished local actor.

And it was awful good 'acting' that helped some Bluffton College football players pull off what has to be the most sportsmen like gesture in the history of college sports in the early 1980s.

After years of dominance behind Elbert's running and Everett's blocking, to help bring more parity to the league, the BC football team went 0-9 in 1983.

"But we were in most of the games," said 'Audi' Jones, still carrying on the ruse all these years later. Audi played split end in 1983.

The fan

Win or lose, Bluffton's Peg Rugley watched Audi's games, as she has watched most every BC college game since, well, anyone can remember. No discourse about BC sports would be complete without her inclusion.

Whether football, basketball, baseball… Peg is there dressed in royal purple and white Bluffton College attire and an over-sized, white cow girl hat – quite vocally cheering the team on.

What's more, Audi said Peg also has this uncanny knack for remembering numbers. And every year on his birthday, or any of the players' birthdays, there would be a phone call of congratulations from Peg.

Someone with almost as much longevity as Peg at BC, is head football coach Carlin Carpenter. He retired this last year after 24 continuous years at BC's helm, a record among Ohio football coaches.

Note: BC's Sports Hall of Fame has glass display cases representing athletes from the various sports, complete with old baseball gloves, deflated footballs and helmets, some with no face masks ("ouch"), volley balls... What's conspicuously missing? Track shoes.

Wrestle Mania (Bluffton-style):'

It was the 'little team' that could...

An absolutely electric time (but no wasted wattage) in Bluffton came in the winter of 1980-'81. The Bluffton High School wrestling team was on track in a big way.

Although often the smallest school in the Invitational meets, they wrestled with skill, a tremendous amount of heart, and success, much success. So much success, that the town started to sense something *special* was about to happen.

"Toward the end of our regular season, we were, amazingly enough, getting more people at the wrestling matches than the basketball team was getting at their games," recalled John Shannon, now owner of Bluffton's Sports Warehouse and one of the stars on that team of yesteryear.

Shannon said the Bluffton crowds increased even more when the team went to the sectionals at Findlay College. And as a show of support, albeit an awfully odd one, BHS parents, and others, started wearing goofy-looking, multi-colored beanies, that were pinned with school buttons and whatnot.

The team won in Findlay then advanced to Bowling Green State University for the Districts, beanies in tow. In Bowling Green they won again, by a quite close 7 and ½ points, according to a *Century of Pirates.*

And the fervor in Bluffton was reaching fever pitch, with everyone abuzz with wrestling talk, from the barber chair at Jerry's, to the halls of the stately Municipal Building, to the restaurant tables, *all* the restaurant tables, throughout town.

And the talk continued, as five of the team members boarded the bus, amidst quite a bit of hoopla, for St. John's Arena in Columbus, and the state finals – where, among others, this unsung Bluffton team would be facing two-time state champions Licking Heights High.

With a sea of Bluffton beanie clad fans looking on at St. John's (one of the strangest sights ever seen in Columbus) the team had at it, fighting and scrapping, taking down and pinning. And when the mat dust cleared, so to speak, John had taken eighth place, three other wrestlers, Don Mathewson, Bill Edwards and Steve Smith, had taken second, and to beat Licking Heights, Mark Falk had to take his final match.

In a nail biter, Mark gutted out a 7-5 victory.

Bluffton had won state, by ½ point!

Shannon said that in their jubilee, the Bluffton parents rented part of a Columbus hotel and threw the kids a big celebration party. Then, recalling it as if it were yesterday, Shannon said the team was met at the Bluffton Village limits by a fire truck escort, and cheering fans lined the streets.

It was now "Bluffton Beanie Mania."

In fact, the beanies would become such a Bluffton collector's item, that John said he was approached by a friend's father who gave him $30 ("...which was a lot of money back then," John smiled) so he could display the Bluffton beanie on his living room mantle.

'Girls of 2000':

It was the '99-2000 season and Bluffton was abuzz, as it had been 20 years earlier for the wrestling team. But this time the excitement centered on the Bluffton High School girl's basketball team.

They had been in the state semi-finals the year before, and all five starters were back – including the Division III Player of the Year Caity Matter.

The Lady Pirates breezed through their season, going 20-0. They then handily won the Sectional, District and Regional competitions. And, once again, a Bluffton team was on the road to Columbus.

With the stands awash in a sea of "Pirate red," but no Bluffton beanies this time – Columbus officials apparently outlawed them after 1980 – the girls took the first game against Eastern Brown, with Matter scoring 32 points.

Then tragedy struck.

In the first minutes of the championship game against South Euclid Regina, Caity hurt her ankle severely. And though the team fought valiantly, including a courageous performance by Caity, they came up short.

The season ended: 26-1.

To find a BHS girl's team with a perfect record, we have to go back – way back.

'Girls of 1913':

Bluffton High School has a tremendously rich history in all sports. In fact, this history has been so noteworthy, *Bluffton News* editor Fred Steiner recently compiled a collection of essays for the book: *A Century of Pirates* (alluded to earlier), which is a fascinating look at Bluffton High School sports over the last 100 years.

And of all these exceptional young athletes, there

were probably none with more grit, more determination, or more cumbersome uniforms, than the BHS girls basketball team of 1913.

According to *A Century of Pirates*, the girls took on all comers (other high schools, colleges or city teams – there was no formal league then) on the second floor of what eventually became the Mastermix Feed Mill here.

Not losing a game in 1913, the *Cleveland Plain Dealer* ran a picture of the team with a challenge to any other girl's team in the state – to meet at a neutral court. One team responded, but apparently wouldn't meet on a neutral floor.

The BHS team automatically declared themselves "state champions."

No brag. Just fact.

'BC's 'Girls of 2003'

Bluffton College women defend against Kentucky's Transylvania College. BC seems to always have a hard time against this team in night games. (photo courtesy of Bluffton College)

In recent weeks as I prepare to write this, in the tradition of the 'BHS Girls of 1913,' the University of Connecticut's girl's basketball team has been on Pg. 1 of sports sections across the country, as they neared, and finally broke, the record for the longest women's basketball college win streak – over 2 years and a phenomenal 55 games.

Conversely, Bluffton College's women's basketball team had been working to *break* a streak – not winning a game the last two years in their Heartland Conference. Our family had been attending most of the women's home games this year (wearing BC royal purple, the whole thing), and we were really pulling for them.

Then, the other night at home in Founders Hall, it happened.

They were playing rival Manchester College. And if you'll allow, for a moment here I'll return to my brief days as sports editor (minus the manual typewriter) of BC's *Witmarsum* student newspaper:

This night, Bluffton got an early lead on some great ball handling and penetration by point guard Karen Harris.

However, toward half-time, Manchester closed the gap.

In the second stanza (sports lingo for second-half), the game see-sawed back and forth, with the BC students exuberantly carrying on, while the professors, just as exuberantly (in their own way, that is) exclaimed things like: "*My*, wasn't that a well executed shot."

At the 5-minute mark, Bluffton went on an 8 point run with some great shooting by senior Lindsey Robinson -- and started to pull away.

The crowd could sense this, finally, was the night.

In fact the game announcer, Kevin Clutz, whose day job is a rather straight-laced hospital administrative one, was so jazzed in the final minutes, that he was seen letting his hair down, *way down*, playing 'air-guitar' under the scorer's table to the *Rocky* movie's *Eye of the Tiger* during a last minute time-out.

At the buzzer, it was Bluffton by 11 – amidst pandemonium. Well OK, maybe not pandemonium, but the student fans were getting a bit raucous and the professors were now exclaiming: "*My*, wasn't that quite a contest."

Note: Even in the BC women's lopsided basketball losses this year, these players never gave up and were always in there scrapping in the final minutes – even when they were down by 25.

And knowing they were doing their best, made the games awful fun to watch, even inspiring.

Because even though it's quite doubtful any of these girls will go on to play in the WBA, they are sports heroes in their own right – and in our seven-year-old Sarah's scrapbook, where she's been pasting pictures of her favorite BC players.

In fact, they are already in 'Sarah's WBA,' and more, could well inspire this little girl to play school basketball someday; but more importantly, these girls' play could well inspire Sarah to never give up, no matter what the score, in life.

The Comeback

In Bluffton College's long line of sports highlights, perhaps there is none more storied (Elbert Dubenion notwithstanding) than, well, mine.

My freshman year I tried out for the junior varsity basketball team at BC. 17 kids tried out. 15 kids were kept.

I wasn't one of them.

Now, pretty sure UCLA wasn't going to call to have me red shirt the following year, you'd think I would have just hung up my high tops.

But not me.

I knew there'd be a BC comeback. And there was.

As I've mentioned, in the year 2001 I 'came back' to Bluffton.

And what's more, now I was being "begged" to play on

the same hardwood I'd left behind some 28 years ago.

A 46-year-old 'phenom,' you wonder?

No. Actually a group of older guys, who were playing at the college gym Mondays and Fridays at 6 a.m.,
had approached me. At that hour, needless to say, they
were always "begging" people to play.

So I laced up my high tops, and, once again, had at
it. And even though I was several years older than the
next youngest guy, I was able to keep up pretty good,
thanks to the miracle of bee pollen and ginseng – plus
we'd only play 45 minutes.

Now even though my "comeback" was, in my estima-
tion, going quite well (although mine by no means was
getting as much press as Michael Jordan's was), the wheels
came off in the third month of the first season.

As a preface, John Schrock, one of the guys who
played with us, is in the wrong sport. Because of his
rather strong, large stature, John would be best suited
for… oh, I don't know… maybe middle linebacker for
the Cleveland Browns, or something.

And it was John who was driving to the hoop this
one particular morning, when I, forgetting I was a few
years removed from my (even mediocre then) point
guard acrobatics of yesteryear, decided to head him off.

I jumped (like a beaver). John kept charging (like a
rhinoceros). And in all that, his shoulder hit my ribs.

The rhinoceros won.

While I played the rest of the game on sheer courage, grit and 'beaver determination,' – plus, the next
basket won -- I had a hard time getting out of bed, or
doing much of anything physical the whole next week.

Now, as I've said, it's a low budget campaign and, I
mean, what can you do for bruised, or broken, ribs anyway, except just wait for them to heal. So I didn't go to

to a doctor, right away.

However, after about a week I was curious, and still in pain.

Since X-rays can be so darn expensive (and I'm not too big on being radiated anyway), I opted for Bluffton's Dr. Terry Chappell.

He's a friend (despite being a University of Michigan fan) and had several times bartered his services for some of Liz's homemade soup. So I stopped by his home late one night and explained to Terry what had happened on the court.

"I just want to know if there's a way to tell if ribs are broken, without having to be X-rayed?" I asked.

Terry, in turn, had me take off my sweater and he began quite deftly, and gingerly, feeling around the area. He gently felt there, then gently there, then suddenly, WITH A WHOLE LOT MORE PRESSURE, he felt *there!*

I jumped (like a kangaroo).

After waiting for me to descend, Terry matter-of-factly concluded:

"Yep, it's definitely broken."

"Eight years of med school for that?!" I laughed, sort of.

Chapter 25

Another 'different' type of Bluffton doctor

Despite his rather unusual rib diagnostics (which, by the way in my case, were right), Dr. Terry Chappell is one of the best doctors in the area, if not in the country. (Thank goodness he didn't transfer to Antarctica too.)

People come from a radius of hundreds of miles to visit Dr. Chappell's somewhat different Celebration of Health Clinic here. They come from all over Ohio, Michigan and Indiana.

The reason they come this far is because Dr. Chappell, a University of Michigan Medical School graduate, combines the best of traditional medicine with many extremely creative alternative ones.

He has spent years exhaustively researching herbal therapies, stress therapies, nutritional therapies… because he said he believes that sometimes just treating the symptoms with traditional medicine is short sighted, and in the long run, can actually be damaging.

As an example, he told me he and his office colleagues often find prescribing red yeast extract (something my diet is definitely short on) will lower cholesterol as effectively, and much safer, than conventional drug treatments – which are often much more expensive and may have side effects.

In line with lower cholesterol, Dr. Chappell is also the author of *Questions from the Heart* (Hampton Roads Publishing), a book about safe alternatives to bypass surgery.

Dr. Chappell has a strong social justice streak as well.

Because many medical expenses have gotten so high and there are many people these days without health insurance (46 million in America), Dr. Chappell runs an Alternative Family Health Care Free Clinic in a depressed part of Lima every Wednesday evening.

One of the things Dr. Chappell tries to get across to the people at this clinic, and at his Bluffton location, is that a main key to good health is nutrition. And he works on a preventative level with his patients to help them reduce sugars, starches, and so on; replacing them with healthier diet items.

But he doesn't stop there.

He also exhorts his patients, and everyone, to reduce their exposure to environmental toxins (yard chemicals, cleaning fluids...). And he gives area seminars and has developed a website (www.healthcelebration.com) to help reinforce this and other health messages.

But he doesn't stop there either.

Dr. Chappel also encourages people to lobby governments, industries and individual consumers to make better decisions about the development and use of things that emit these toxins.

Upon hearing Dr. Chappell's multi-dimensional approach to healing people, and society, I couldn't help but think he would make a great Surgeon General under our administration.

"Average Joe" platform point: "If people ate better, were less stressed, had less toxins, and exercised more – well, they wouldn't get sick as much."

Well, it's true.

Chapter 26

The food we eat...

As basic to quality of life is the air we breath, so too is the "food we eat," and sometimes grow.

Many people in Bluffton are quite health conscious about the food they eat. And more, many also see a connectedness to the earth, and each other, as vital parts of the "food chain" continuum as well.

To this end, Bluffton, for one, is very 'garden oriented.'

For instance, Bluffton has two community gardens.

Some of the enthusiasm for these gardens, and gardening in general, comes from a quite active Garden Club.

Besides members' individual gardens, the club has been busy around town helping creatively landscape Bluffton's Middle School, coordinating beautification projects at the town's parks, and so on.

Garden Club vice-president Becky Ahmed told me the group also meets once a month throughout the year to learn about an array of things. Over this last winter, for instance, one of the months they learned about tapping maple sugar. (Bluffton astronomer Ron Rich taps one of his Maple trees out back every year.)

Becky also said on another month, the group met at Maple Crest Nursing Complex here to paint designs on clay pots.

During the summers, besides taking field trips to other gardening projects in Northwest Ohio, club members are quite prolific with their own gardens.

Bluffton's Best

A garden that is perhaps the best in Bluffton, not to mention (although you knew I would) best in the country, is Linda and Hans Houshower's on Washington, Ave.

Looking like something out of *Gardening Magazine*, the Houshower's garden has lush rows of asparagus, raspberries, strawberries, melons, tomatoes, beans, cucumbers... you name it.

They even have a rather rare, for this climate zone, Asian pear-apple tree (just yet another example of Bluffton 'diversity').

"They (pear-apples) sell for a buck a piece at the grocery," Linda smiled about her significant savings.

What adds dramatically to the quality of the pear-apples, and the garden produce, is rich compost the Houshower's get free, as do other community members, from Bluffton's huge compost pile, made every year from a mixture of leaves and wood collected throughout town during the fall.

And while the *real* John Deere's (minus the beaver) can be seen in the area fields during late night plantings, their powerful head lights on; so too can Linda often be seen late nights with her car headlights on, mixing in the compost and rushing to also make planting season.

The Houshower's also grow everything organically.

In fact, Linda is such a big proponent of healthy food, she and her husband, with Jon and Sally Sommer, opened a Whole Food Market downtown in 1984.

The store sells organic rice, flour, beans...

Over Ceylon Mango tea (*well, I don't just drink coffee*), Linda told me that a study at the turn of the 1900s showed an average person's body tissue ("average" being the mean across a lot of study subjects) had about 12 chemicals, at most. Now it's 200.

And to make matters worse, Linda explained studies also show it is the interaction of these chemicals (pesticides, fertilizers, hormones fed to animals...) in the body that are causing cancer, or other diseases.

And, it is some of these same chemicals that are destroying the soil.

Garden Co-op

Bluffton's Ray Person and Elizabeth Kelly believe it's not our role to destroy the soil, or any part of nature. They, instead, believe we are to be good stewards of the environment.

Ray is a professor of religion at nearby Ohio Northern University and Elizabeth is a hospital chaplain.

At the coffee hour, after one of the First Mennonite Church's weekly Tuesday morning prayer services, Elizabeth told me her and her husband Ray are concerned about the rapidly increasing loss of the family farm in America as well. And to help reverse the trend, they have recently bought a 20-acre farm in the country here.

Some 13 acres are leased to a local farmer and several acres of the Person's farm have been put aside for an organic garden Co-op.

Several families will share labor, equipment, cost of seeds... in a gardening and community-building effort.

In addition, the Persons have set up a "Summer Kitchen" in their garage (complete with stove, refrigerator, sink...) for joint canning, and other projects.

(To be even better stewards of the environment, the Persons have also gone to a non-polluting, and quite efficient, corn burning stove, and they have also installed a compost toilet.)

Farmer's Market

If there is an over-flow of produce from the garden Co-op, a home for these veggies may well become the new weekly Farmer's Market in downtown Bluffton.

A project of the Bluffton Area Chamber of Commerce, Bluffton's Farmer's Market will be staged every Saturday morning between May and October.

Besides stands of fruit, produce and homemade food ("...with an emphasis on organic"), there will also be music and cooking displays.

Along with the emphasis on food products using natural materials, the market will provide a direct link to local growers – enhancing community building even that much more.

Community Sponsored Agriculture

One of the farmers the market will have a direct link to is TR Steiner and his nearby Red Oak Run Farms.

TR has also just started a Community Sponsored Agriculture project to further help reconnect local people with local food – like in the old days.

"With produce (now) traveling thousands of miles from field to table, we've lost the connection between local farm, land and consumer," said TR.

Community members will be offered "shares" ($390 a full share, $200 a half). In return, shareholders will receive weekly produce from TR's farm.

What's more, if a full shareholder chooses to work 10 hours on the farm, they get $100 off, and for five hours of work, a half shareholder gets $50 off.

"People say that's generous," said TR. "But I think farm labor should be viewed as a valuable thing in our society.

A member of First Mennonite Church, TR said nothing from the farm will get wasted, with overflow produce going to a Soup Kitchen in Lima.

Note: Bluffton College sponsors a weekly Forum Series, bringing in experts on any number of

topics.   The college recently had Amish author
David Kline in to talk about small farming.   Kline
said if you ride down most of Ohio's rural roads between June and August what you'll see is: nothing.
That is, no one out in the fields.   With mechaniza-
tion, chemical weed killers and pesticides, "...you
plant in the spring and harvest in the fall," said
Kline.   He continued the variety of things that used
to normally go on in the fields (continual tilling,
planting, weeding...), helped farmers stay in touch
with the soil, with themselves and with God.   A sad
contemporary commentary, Kline said it's been
suggested if a modern 'mechanized' farmer wants to
stay in touch with the soil these days: "They should
work in their wife's garden."

Kline is the editor of *Farming Magazine* and a series of books.

Bluffton Books:

Speaking of books...

For a small town, Bluffton has the best collection of
libraries anywhere.

The library at First Mennonite Church, for instance,
is run like a regular library.   It's staffed by six volunteers and it's required you check books out.   If you're
late returning them, you pray, instead of pay.   (Don't
laugh, a library in southern Ohio has people pay late
fines in cans of food for the local food pantry.)

Theme book displays change monthly at First
Mennonite and, in general, they have quite an as-
sortment of books on spirituality, peace and social
justice... for adults and children.   For the kids and I,
the Children's Section here has become our Sunday
afternoon reading spot – although I have the darndest

time sitting in those little chairs.

Mary Lou Verclear explained congregation members donate new, or "like new" books regularly, and the church also allocates for their yearly operating budget.

To the west is Bluffton College's Musselman Library, open to both students and the public.

Besides a wonderful array of books, and an extremely helpful staff, this library has the nicest reading room of any college in the country.

On days when it's sunny in Bluffton (which is always), light streams in through gaping, Georgian-style arched windows in Musselman's reading room, washing over long oak tables and high back, stately oak chairs.

Out those Georgian-style windows is a view of the bronze sculpture: "Constellation Earth." The sculpture depicts young adults suspended in air, clasping hands as they circle the globe, performing, in essence, a cosmic 'swirl' of life.

And also, as sculpture figures sometimes are "for the ('dubious,' my emphasis) sake of art," these young adults are unclothed.

As an aside, to give you an example of the level, and nature, of vandalism on campus, one day last year the campus awoke to see the Constellation Earth sculpture had been, not so much defaced, as 'artistically compromised.' (The more modest leaning of us in town thinking perhaps compromised for the better.)

The figures had all been clothed: in diapers.

Several blocks east of the college library, the town library is also being 'dressed up' with some major renovation and expansion in the wake of a recently approved library levy.

Besides a tremendously improved facility, Bluffton-Richland Public Library has what I thought was the country's friendliest librarians.

Recently however, not so much by crack journalism techniques, as by sheer happenstance, I found differently.

I had gone into the library's back office to consult with computer expert Gail Neff, when I noticed a rather telling, and rather large, wall sign. It read:

"We appreciate all our patrons. Some when they come; and some when they go."

I pointed to the sign and asked a group of librarians congregated in one corner of the room:

"Which am I?"

Silence.

"No *really* guys, which am I?"

More silence.

Chapter 27

'World Walking,'
Hugh Downs Style

Hugh Downs (photo courtesy of Bluffton College)

Speaking of journalism…

One of the top TV journalists ever, Hugh Downs, at-tended Bluffton College for his freshman year (1938-39.)

In a *Lima News* interview once, Downs, like my-self (small world, huh), said later in life he had a different perspective of his education at BC than he had when he was a student.

"I don't think I appreciated it when I was here," he said.

But he has since come to appreciate it in such a way that he has served as Honorary National Campaign Chairman for BC's *Share the Vision Campaign*, and has spoken at several Bluffton College Commencements.

Downs, like Phyllis Diller, grew up in Lima, Ohio. He went to BC that freshman year, after winning a public speaking contest.

Because of finances, Downs then returned to Lima where he worked at WLOK radio as a "cub announcer." He soon moved to Chicago to announce for the "Kukla, Fran and Ollie Show." Then moved to New York where he announced for the Tonight Show and Concentration.

He left television in 1971 to pursue personal interests, then returned in 1978 to host the popular ABC News "20/20" show.

One of Down's "personal interests," in the tradition of BC's brand of social justice, is helping others internationally. He's gotten behind UNICEF projects to help bring water to drought stricken areas of Africa, projects to get food and medicine to Haiti...

In 1987, he was given a Human Rights Award by a United Nations Association in Arizona.

It was that same year, Downs came to BC to kick off the Share the Vision Campaign and relate a personal anecdote that he considers his "most memorable moment."

It was December 10, 1982. That was the day he moved the South Pole marker and proceeded to walk around the world – in 24 steps.

The *Lima News* reported Downs had long been interested in making an Antarctic Expedition. (It just seems to be something that happens to some people when they come to Bluffton.)

After scientists discovered that the marker at the pole was slightly off center (probably hit by an "ice-biker"), Downs was given permission to film the moving of the pole marker for the "20/20" show.

When Downs arrived, he, unexpectedly, was given the honor of moving the pole.

According to the article, Downs moved the pole 10 meters, then paced off seven steps back. He then "walked around the world in 24 steps," with each step in a different time zone.

(If only Bluffton 'globejogger' Paul Klassen had thought about this, huh. He probably wouldn't have pulled even half the muscles he did.)

And I also have to say here, what is it anyway about these Bluffton people wanting to go around the world, one way or the other?

Now you'd think the oddity, per capita, of two Blufftonites being connected to circling the world in such spectacular, or at least 'out of the ordinary' ways, would be all that local lore could support – or that I could credibly put in this book.

But, 'incredibly,' it's not.

Through more crack investigative work, and sheer dumb luck, I met Darcy Newman. Her name wasn't always Newman.

Darcy Dill played point guard for the women's BC basketball team and was First Team All Ohio as a short-stop for the BC women's slow-pitch softball team. One year her batting average was a phenomenal 682.

Darcy also majored in education and graduated in 1984. She then went on to Brown County, Ohio, to teach.

After several years there, she met Steve Newman, a tall

lanky guy, with a great smile – and quite calloused feet.

On their first date, Darcy learned those calloused feet had been formed over four years – which is how long it had taken Steve to be the first one, and still the only one (not counting Hugh Downs), to solo-walk the world.

And he did it, not as Bluffton's Paul Klassen had done it, but Steve actually walked through a bunch of countries, seven continents, the whole thing. (See: www.theworldwalker.com)

Having lived in Bluffton, once Darcy found out Steve had walked the world, she instantly fell in love and they soon were 'walking' (sorry) down the aisle.

My theory

"Constellation Earth." Sculpture a bit out of focus, on purpose. (photo by Joe Schriner)

Now I have a theory on all this: "Constellation Earth," the BC sculpture I mentioned earlier that depicts students reaching to clasp hands as they swirl around the globe, is, I believe, sending subliminal messages to other Blufftonites to do the same. What's more, the figures, being unclothed the way they are, obviously get cold sometimes. And to get people to empathize with their plight, it's also my belief they are sending more subliminal messages (piggybacking onto, like, the air waves of the campus radio station) for people to go to places that are: cold. And thus we have the.Bluffton exodus to: Antarctica.

Case closed. (Because Liz said I had to stop now.)

Communications:

Speaking of the BC campus radio station...

When Hugh and I ("Hugh and I," nice ring to it, huh.) went to school at Bluffton College, there was no Communication Department. There is now. The department offers students education in print, photography and broadcast journalism.

In fact, Bluffton's campus radio, WBCR, where many of these students get experience, is currently changing from AM to FM. Its signal will now be broadcast to towns as far away as Ada and Pandora -- about a 50-mile radius. (When I was a student here, WBCR's signal barely made it to the dorms on the outskirts of campus.)

For BC history buffs, WBCR's first even weaker signal, was broadcast in the 1950s when a student placed on antenna on top of College Hall. While not confirmed, it is believed a *Witmarsum* college newspaper reporter here has genealogically linked this particular student with one of the "5-watt Christmas engineers" over on Sunset St.

Many journalism students at BC get valuable experience writing for the *Witmarsum*, which was named after a small town in the province of Friesland, Holland. (Nobody seems to know why.)

Now while the newspaper doesn't cover this town (I checked), it does cover BC's campus scene and runs a variety of news, editorials and features.

Perhaps the most read feature revolves around a question of the week which is posed to, not the "man-on-the-street," but rather the "beaver-on-the-street." (I'm sorry, but I think what we've got here is a case of Orwellian *1984* 'beaverthink.')

Anyway, the question that was asked last week was: "What does the word 'oeillade" mean?"

Beaver-on-the-street Ben Graber, who apparently is majoring in biology, answered: "It's a sponge that lives on the ocean floor that wears pants." (That would have been my guess.)

The newspaper is often colloquially abbreviated "The Wit" around campus. And now you know why.

Incidentally, upon checking, I found oeillade actually isn't even a word.

Nuts. With thingamabob *and* oeillade, I would have been unbeatable at Scrabble.

Bluffton News:

Besides the *Witmarsum*, the other newspaper in town is the weekly *Bluffton News* (mentioned several times earlier). The newspaper recently won two state wide awards for editorial page pieces by *News* editor Fred Steiner. This is the 7th year in a row the newspaper has received awards at the Buckeye Press Association Show in Columbus. The *News* recently celebrated its 125th year.

Writer's group:

Another writing outlet that's been around for many

years in Bluffton is the town's Writer's Group. Elaine Sommers Rich said the group meets once a month and the format includes: bringing in outside authors to talk; readings; and, a time for group members to report on any of their recent writing sales. Elaine, in fact, has been quite vocal during these segments, having placed numerous newspaper and magazine pieces, as well as publishing eight books. Liz and Sarah are currently quite engrossed in Elaine's book: *Hannah Elizabeth*, a story of a young Mennonite girl coming of age. The book is available at First Mennonite's Church library and was published in 1964.

A book that was published this year, *Anthology of Poetry by Young Americans*, contains a phenomenal 45 poems by students in Robin Ault's language arts classes at Bluffton Middle School.

Used Books

And if you're looking for even more books in Bluffton, Book ReViews, Et Cetera, a used bookstore on Main St., just recently opened. The store is a Mennonite outreach, with profits going to the Mennonite Central Committee.

Owner Ruth Unrau, told me she is a retired English professor who said she and her husband, Walter, wanted to stay active through meaningful volunteer work. (The couple has also done missionary work in India, and Ruth is the author of: *Hill Station Teacher (a life with India in it)*.

Ruth said her store has a wide variety of books (fiction, non-fiction, biography cooking, religion, travel...). It even has a children's room called: Pooh's Corner.

Books are donated, or traded, with Ruth advising that underlining sometimes "makes the books more noteworthy."

Chapter 28

Running Dog With Monkey

Speaking of "noteworthy"…

In the essay before last, I mentioned the "Constellation Earth" sculpture.

There's more.

Bluffton College has recently added a Centennial Sculpture Garden with the inclusion of seven rather impressive pieces by artists who all have ties to the college.

There is, for instance, BC professor Greg Luginbuhl's *The Last First Draft*, depicting a handwritten manuscript, complete with "letters, doodles and margin illustrations" representing thoughts behind the words.

The "paper" is a thick, bronze slab positioned almost 'tauntingly' adjacent to BC's high tech computer lab.

I'm particularly partial to professor Luginbuhl's piece because this manuscript, like almost all I write, was initially done in a hand written fashion – although on a lot lighter paper, and with more "doodles."

A little ways up from the *Last Draft* sculpture, is a sculpture of what appears to be an exhausted man and his horse, both struggling to ascend a hill. It's titled: *Reaching Their Goal One Step at a Time.*

Artist Mary Kline Roynesdal '80, explained completing a mountaineering course at Bluffton College taught her that anything she started (even when it looked impossible) could be completed "one step at a time."

Just beyond this sculpture is a sculpture with figures that don't appear as tired, but one looks rather 'burdened.' It is the sculpture of a sleek, extremely fast looking dog (resembling a skinny greyhound), running with a monkey on it's back.

It's titled: *Running Dog With Monkey*.

Now I'm not sure how many actual seconds it took sculptor, and BC art instructor Jaye Bumbaugh to come up with that title; but his explanation of what the piece symbolizes, I'm guessing, might have taken a bit longer, and ties in quite nicely with the college's ethos of diversity.

"...to live together in harmony, we must find ways to deal with the disparities among us; the unexpected; the surprises; the monkeys on the backs of dogs," professor Bumbaugh explains.

Now if I may (Liz is out of the room) wax interpretive once again: While what the professor describes is admittedly quite thoughtful and deep, I have to say I see this piece at even a deeper level of symbolism.

Really taking the time to contemplate the sculpture one day over some Frangelica blend coffee, it all became eminently clear.

The fast dog is the symbolic embodiment of every BC sprinter who has ever donned a pair of track shoes here. The monkey on the dog's back, slowing it down? Yep, *the beaver.*

Besides this symbolic representation, up the path from the Centennial Sculpture Garden there is an actual small sculpture of "the beaver." And near that, is a statue of "the Kobzar."

This is a stone statue of a Ukrainian folk minstrel, former BC art professor J.P. Klassen saw performing in an opera house in St. Petersburg. The statue was offered to the Russian people as a gift because they had been hospitable to the Mennonites, but it was refused because the Russians were afraid of rekindling Ukrainian Nationalism.

Nevertheless, the statue is symbolic of bridging the gap between Mennonite and non-Mennonite people.

It is so strong a symbol on campus, that when Professor Perry Bush wrote a book about the history of Bluffton College for its 100th anniversary in 1999, it was titled: *Dancing with Kobzar.*

When Liz came back in the room, I told her I found myself writing so much about Bluffton College for this book, I was thinking about a title that would have a serial quality in relation to Professor Bush's historical tome. That's right: *Dances With Beavers.*

I told her I thought if Hugh Downs asked Kevin Costner, nicely...

Liz then left the room again.

Hugh Downs, Part 2:

The Kobzar statue sits right in front of the Marbeck Center. In 1968, Hugh Downs had come to BC to give a speech to about 1,000 people gathered for the dedication of the Marbeck Center, the college's new Student Union. It is reported he did it for good-will, alumni-type reasons.

The kids and I think he did it for the ice cream cones.

On the lower level of the Marbeck Center is The Barn Restaurant. It's got a grill, some chips and *great* ice cream cones, 55 cents. *(Is Bluffton stuck in a time warp, or what?)*

As a family treat, we will take the kids down here on a Saturday afternoon. Although for the last six months, The Barn has been closed as the Marbeck Center goes through its own major renovation and expansion.

Meanwhile, we've been going through our own: ice cream withdrawal.

Note: Come spring, not only will The Barn be re-opened for ice cream, but the Dairi Freeze on South Main Street opens as well for the season.

The Dairi Freeze is your basic small town, well, Dairi Freeze. It's housed in small, non-descript (except when it had the black velvet Elvis posters a couple years ago) square brick building. And typical of these places, it's got outside tables that are always filled every day it gets above 80 degrees.

What's not typical about this Dairi Freeze, in fact it's probably the only one in the country that does this, is they let you to pick an ice cream topping, and a cause, with your order.

That is, various town organizations are on a big poster out front and the store pledges to donate 10% of a purchase to the cause of your choice.

Some of the organizations include: the High School Music Department; EMS Services; High School swim team; youth groups... And here's an oxymoron. One of the other Dairi Freeze choices: the local chapter of TOPS (Take Off Pounds Sensibly).

I'm told the TOPS people are particularly partial to the sugar free / fat free ice cream. Although I couldn't help but think: 'Sugar free, fat free – what's the point?'

Chapter 29

Painter's Plus Pause

A 'weird something'

Speaking of 'what's the point?'…

Dale Way asked me to help him with a job on County Road 103 in rural Bluffton. It was a job I am, perhaps, best suited for in the handyman field: holding a ladder.

A globe in a street-light looking fixture, high over a farm house had gone out. It wasn't the first time the light had gone out at this particular location.

Dale told me a couple years back he had been called here to replace the same light. His side-kick Greg Mohr was, this time, holding the ladder, as Dale precariously balanced on the top rung of his high-extension ladder in a pretty brisk wind.

It was tense.

However, something would soon happen to break the tension in a most odd way.

While reaching to screw the new light in, Dale, by happenstance, turned to glance at a pick-up truck speeding by. The pick-up then, without any apparent warning, broke hard, tires fish tailing and screeching loudly.

The driver then slammed the vehicle into reverse and sped quite a ways backward, making a hard turn into the driveway and coming to an abrupt stop just before the garage.

Dale was now able to recognize local Dr. Harold Barleycamp. Dr. Barleycamp proceeded to hurriedly jump out, sprint toward Dale and Greg, stop, and holler:

"HEY! DO YOU GUYS NEED A TROMBONE PLAYER?"

In the absurdity of the moment, Dale and Greg didn't have an immediate response. And Dr. Barleycamp didn't particularly wait for one.

He just as quickly turned, raced back to his vehicle and was off like a shot in the direction he'd been going.

After trying, quite unsuccessfully, to make sense of the story, I asked Dale.

"Why did Dr. Barleycamp do that?"

"I don't know. He's just like that," Dale replied.

Dale then started to climb toward the light, leaving me, in essence, in the dark. Although at least now I did have something, albeit a 'weird something,' to think about while I was holding the ladder.

What is it about these Bluffton doctors anyway?

Chapter 30

An outlet for their youth

Apparently in touch with his "inner trombonist," what Dr. Barleycamp did that day in rural Bluffton could best be characterized as something we are more likely to see in the cavalier moments of youth.

Speaking of youth... *(Well, **you** try to keep making these transitions!)*

During our Campaign 2000 travels, we met a man in Arthur, Illinois, who had helped start a baseball league for youth in the town.

He told us town quality of life has a lot to do with how the adults in a town offer the next generation an "outlet for their youth."

And Bluffton does this well.

Besides those already mentioned, Bluffton High School has a number of other programs to help students develop their talents and interests. Among the clubs BHS offers: Spanish Club, Latin Club, SADD (Students Against Destructive Decisions) Club, Math Club, Art Club, Computer clubs, Science Club, Academic Team...

Envirothon Team

Of all the Bluffton High School teams (football, basketball, baseball...) that have made it to the state finals in Columbus, the team that's been there the most has been (surprise): the Envirothon Team.

They have, in fact, been to the Columbus finals six times in the past eight years – with some pretty stiff competition just from the 80 teams in their regional Northwest Ohio Division.

Team advisor JoAnn Antibus said each year Envirothon Clubs nationwide are given an environmental topic to research. They look at the "good and bad aspects" of different ecological phenomena.

JoAnn said this year the team was looking at farmland preservation. In other years, they've looked at the ozone, wetlands, urbanization…

In the year 2001, Bluffton's research work concerning "no-point source pollution" (pollution entering streams through farming, oil on roadways, pesticides…) gained them a stellar third place in Ohio.

"Betel Guese"

JoAnn Antibus is also the advisor for the Bluffton High School Science Olympiad Team, which recently brought home six medals from the annual Regional Science Competition in Lima.

Among these medals was a second place for Cody Ault and Clay Haymes' "Astronomy Project." (Since Professor Ron Rich has diminished some of the light pollution in town, many people have turned back to astronomy.)

JoAnn said Cody and Clays' project looked at star constellations, one of the most noted being Orion (which astronomers say if the 'star dots' were connected, appears to form the picture of a prehistoric "hunter.")

JoAnn said one of the most well-known stars in Orion is: Betel Guese (pronounced, "Beetle Juice," she said.).

When asked what the name meant, JoAnn said it was Arabic for: "Arm Pit." That is, this particular star marks just about where the "hunter's" arm pit is.

Academic Team

Carrying on the tradition of excellence at Bluffton High School, the Academic Team recently earned two league championships and qualified for regional competition for the third year in a row. In fact, the brain trust is so good with the Academic Team (probably the best in the country for their age), that our "average Joe" Presidential Committee tapped one of the members, Ross Hughes, to be a campaign consultant.

Sadly, we had to limit Ross's participation once he started consistently using more than three syllable words during the strategy meetings. However, Ross did redeem himself, quite admirably, at an "average Joe" fundraiser by displaying, not so much his intellectual prowess, as he did a kind of odd ambidextrous one.

He played the ukulele behind his back.

Drama Club

Bluffton High School's Drama Club, which puts on a wonderful variety of performances each year for the town, just finished *Go Ask Alice* – a '60s drama about a young girl's descent into drugs.

Mari Way, Dale's daughter, played Alice.

The week her picture was featured in the *Bluffton News*, in connection with *Go Ask Alice*, I saw Mari at a First Mennonite Church potluck.

I approached Mari. And in an attempt to stay in step with Bluffton humor standards, I inquired:

"So Mari, what are we supposed to 'ask' you?"

"*Oh Mr. Schriner*, you're like the fifth person to say that this week," Mari smiled, rolling here eyes.

I could only hope the town doesn't 'ask' me to leave.

Chapter 31

Bluffton Family Recreation

In 1978, a group of citizens were concerned there was not enough organized activities for youth in town. So an ad hoc committee formed a non-profit Bluffton Family Recreation (BFR) organization.

They began using church basements, elementary school gyms and halls for a variety of sports and other activities for youth. With a small stipend, a coordinator was also hired. And it grew.

By the early '90s, it was clear the BFR needed its own facility, said director Carol Enneking. And the community responded.

Land was acquired. Local fundraising ensued. And when the building started, local people helped with some of the construction.

The initial building was completed in 1995. It had basketball courts, aerobic rooms and so on. An expansion project in 2000 added an indoor soccer arena, walking track and fitness center.

The most recent listing of BFR activities included: tennis, volley ball, tumble and dance, yoga, soccer, karate, Swiss ball toning (not an Olympic sport, yet).

Carol said the BFR runs on donations, membership fees and volunteer help.

The facility also hosts all types of sports leagues for youth.

Assistant coach Lisa Wenger had two daughters, ages 10 and 12, playing on the Spartans team this year. They, like BC's track team, won some, lost some.
But more importantly, Lisa told me the games are great exercise for the kids and go a long way in helping them build self esteem.

Lisa also noted every game was quite well attended by town adults.

All that sort of mountain stuff

Some of the town adults also reach beyond the city limits here to help youth.

Bluffton College social work Professor Don Brubaker told me he and an ONU student from Hoytville, Ohio, developed a mentoring program for youth in Toledo.

Volunteer adults pair with youth on a week-long trip to the mountains of New Hampshire. They would climb, repel and all that sort of mountain stuff that requires a good amount of team work.

In all this, Professor Brubaker said bonding and trust grew.

Back in the city after the experience, some youth were now more apt to go to their mentors for advice, support. The program requires a year commitment from each mentor, but for many it's grown to be longer.

Back in Bluffton, there are a variety of excellent youth programs at the Bluffton Public library.

Also, Bluffton has many Boy Scout, Girl Scout and Royal Rangers (Christian equivalent of Boy & Girl Scouts) troops. To give you an idea of the town support for these kids, local Girl Scout "Cookie Coordinator" mom Amy Marcum recently reported just two troupes of some 20 girls sold almost 3,500 Girl Scout cookies during a recent drive.

That's almost a cookie per person in Bluffton!

And this Girl Scout industriousness is not just being channeled into the sale of cookies either. If the truth be known, the Bluffton Girl Scouts have become some of my top foreign affairs consultants.

"Green, green grass."

Last year, George W. Bush had just gotten back from a week long swing through Asia, stopping in Japan, South Korea and China.

Not to be outdone, I visited six countries – in one day.

Bluffton's Annual Girl Scout Day, held at the Methodist Church, traditionally features displays and presentations about different countries around the world.

Our daughter Sarah's troupe did Ireland where there's "…green, green grass," said Sarah. (I bet George W. doesn't even know that.)

Another troupe explained in Sweden that there's no division between Girl Scouts and Boy Scouts, everyone ties knots together.

I also learned they eat Chinchilla's in Chile; and, a Girl Scout explained in Chile's recent history a scare there was cyanide in some of their grape exports devastated an already fragile economy there.

Bluffton outreach

The evening of the same day I attended the Girl Scout event in Bluffton, St. Mary's Church here hosted a Social Justice Night with a talk by a priest who used to have a parish in, of all places, Chile.

Fr. Thom Hemm said he saw first hand how the grape problem talked about at the Girl Scout event had wreaked havoc on Chile.

To make matters worse, Fr. Hemm said in Chile (and throughout the Third World), "cards in general are

stacked against the poor." He cited years of political
and economic oppression as examples.

What's more, he said, companies from wealthier countries, like America, have a tendency to exploit a poorer
country's natural resources and their labor forces.

Fr. Hemm also said he watched horrified as School of
America trained militia worked to undermine a government in Chile that had been favorable to the poor, but not
necessarily favorable to U.S. interests there (both political
and economic).

Fr. Hemm acknowledged many average U.S. citizens
are unaware of this off shore, military maneuvering; or for
that matter, have much of a real understanding of the level
of poverty people in the Third World face.

His solution, he said, is for Americans to enter into
"solidarity" with the poor throughout the world. Fr.
Hemm said in some cases this means working "elbow to
elbow" with the poor.

To that end, his current church, SS. Peter and Paul in
Ottawa, Ohio, has established a sister church project with a
church in rural Guatemala, with parishioners traveling
down to work side by side.

Likewise, First Mennonite Church in Bluffton has developed a sister-church relationship with Colonia Lopez
Mennonite Church in the Honduras, with members traveling there to help.

Bluffton's English Lutheran Church is part of a 'sister-
synod' outreach to the Doma Diocese in Tanzania.

David Runk, president of English Lutheran's Church
Council, told me his church helps Tanzania through a be-
nevolent fund. And he said church members also travel to
Haiti to help with the building of churches and schools
there.

"These are our Christian brothers and sisters who are
facing a lot of things (poverty, religious persecution...)
that we in America don't face as much of. We must help,"
said David.

Note: In yet another strategy to help end world poverty, Bluffton College has given an International scholarship to Jean-Paul Tiendrebeogo. He is from the African country Burkina-Faso, which is about the geographic size of Ohio and has 12 million people. Jean Paul told me poverty is staggering there, and because of poor nutrition, poor health care, and so on, the average life-span in Burkina-Faso is merely 40 years – almost half that of America. Jean-Paul told me he has come here to learn as much as possible about economic systems, agricultural systems, health care systems... so he can take them back to his country to help. And ideally, he said he thought he'd be most effective doing that by becoming president of the country. And he's got a good start: This year he was elected president of the Junior Class at BC.

Chapter 32

"Only have a cardboard box."

In the spirit of Jean-Paul Tiendrebeogo and the Bluffton churches, and as a show of "solidarity" with refugees around the world, Bluffton College's Peace Club camped in 12 degree March weather recently, fasted on liquids for five days and raised money and awareness. What's more, their efforts also sparked an impromptu "tent city," as a number of families in Bluffton started to join them.

As part of Justice Week, a yearly tradition at BC, Peace Club students petitioned their classmates, raising $2,000 – which would cover the entire cost of building a new house for a displaced family in Afghanistan.

Just back from a "Border Tour" to look at poverty and Hispanic immigration issues in Juarez, Mexico, our family joined this year's Bluffton tent city. And when a *Lima News* reporter asked our Sarah, then 6, why she was at the event, Sarah replied:

"We should be grateful just to have a tent, because some people only have a cardboard box." (Sarah had apparently been paying close attention in Juarez.)

BC's Matt Francis has been paying close attention too.

"A lot of innocent people are losing their homes and their lives (worldwide)," Francis told me. "We can't forget, and have to do all we can to help."

BC student Kristen Stager said while the BC tent city didn't simulate the long-term conditions refugees go through, there were some short-term parallels in the temporary absence of a home, heat and regular meals.

"This went beyond the abstract to the experiential," said professor Perry Bush, who is the BC Peace Club advisor.

"You really learn about land mines…"

In tandem with trying to help stop Third World poverty, as wars rage around the globe, BC's Peace Club is trying to help promote peace.

Also recently, the Peace Club, in conjunction with BC in general, sponsored a two-day "Building Cultures of Peace" seminar that brought educators and students from around the country together to talk about terror, war and cutting edge ways to promote peace.

Keynote speaker Andrew Rice, a member of the "Sept. 11 Families for Peaceful Tomorrows" told me his brother David was on the 104th floor of the second World Trade Center Tower the day terror struck.

After a plane hit the first tower, Andrew said his brother called home.

"He was calm and said people in their building were told to stay inside because of the danger of the falling debris," said Andrew.

Then the other plane hit. David died in the raging inferno that ensued.

Andrew said while he felt a lot of anger at his brother's death, instead of wanting revenge, he would rather see more focus on the promotion of non-violence.

And it's that focus that drives Lisa Schirch, a professor at Eastern Mennonite University in Harrisonburg, Virginia, who was also a keynote speaker at the conference. Ms. Schirch said her university's Peace Studies Program draws Fulbright Scholars from Israel, Palestine, Africa, India… to learn about non-violence and conflict resolution so they can take the techniques back to their homeland.

As mentioned earlier, BC offers its students the opportunity to go to these others' "homelands" to work side-by-side for peace and social justice through the Cross Cultural Program.

"That's when you *really* learn about land mines, you *really* learn about poverty," said BC professor Dan Wessner at the conference.

Wessner also added BC has recently gotten a large grant from the Lilly Foundation for their "Pathways Program," which focuses on the college's promotion of peace, cross cultural education and ministry studies.

Peace Center:

Another place to "study peace," is the College's Lion and Lamb Peace Center, which was briefly alluded to earlier. The Peace Center has an extensive library of books about various cultures, peace building, and so on, for youth and adults. And this, too, is open to the public.

The Center is also filled with extremely stirring cross-cultural art.

For instance, a Floyd Cooper drawing of generations of a black family silhouetted against a tree on the water's bank, is accompanied by a line from a Joyce Carol Thomas poem:

"...I look across water and cry for our trembling family tree."

Then there is a bronze and wood sculpture depicting a Native American grandmother on the tragic Trail of Tears; a painting of a young Hiroshima girl affected by the atom bomb, a "Kid's Wall" bronze sculpture of children helping children; "Sadie's Peace Quilt" designed after a Bluffton artist, Sally Lehman, observed the Gulf War... and so many other pieces.

Meanwhile, a striking "Peace Wall" stands outside the Center. Designed as an interactive art experience, the wall replicates part of the Berlin Wall, political prison walls and the Vietnam War Memorial.

Peace Wall designer Jon Barlow Hudson said he wants visitors to think: "...how we close people out, or hold others in, with walls of various kinds."

The Peace Center hosts workshops and puts on trainings around peace and conflict resolution, and a variety of other subjects, for schools, civic groups and so on.

Peace Heroes:

As an alternative to Halloween, the Peace Center recently hosted a "Kid's Café," with community children coming to the event dressed as their favorite "Peace Hero."

Sarah went as her guardian angel, Liz went as the Blessed Virgin Mary, and a man in his mid-70s, Bluffton's Darvin Luginbuhl, went as a hobo.

The featured speaker this day, Darvin said his grandfather was his "peace hero" because, even though he had nine children, he still kept the "tramp room" empty.

Darwin told the kids during the late 1800s the grandfather lived on a railway line on the outskirts of Bluffton and he would regularly take hobos who rode the rails in. He offered free room and board, and would sometimes find them jobs. These men were often immigrants trying to get a start, said Darvin.

Kid's Café coordinator (Who else?) Wendy Chappell-Dick told the rather large group gathered this day that we all had to remember:

"If we want peace in the world, it has to be modeled by each parent in the home."

Chapter 33

'The 'Big Blue Penguin'

Close to where I believe Darvin Luginbuhl's grandfather lived by the tracks, stands a train depot. Yet another Bluffton train depot.

An old Northern Ohio RR building, it has since changed hands.

In recent years, this building on North Main St. has been turned into a restaurant through a fabulous renovation project. True to the building's old character, there are pictures of old trains and railroad maps on the walls. There are old, restored train signal lights. Everything.

The owners of the depot building, after careful deliberation, and what I have to believe was some lengthy discussion with BC art professor Jay Bumbaugh ("Running Dog With Monkey"), decided to call the establishment: The Depot.

Now what the name lacks in imagination, the cuisine makes up for. Especially the frozen yogurt.

And it was ice cream cones the kids, their neighborhood friends, and I were having after one of our spirited back yard soccer matches.

While I wasn't in the habit of regularly taking the *whole* neighborhood gang to the Depot, this was a special day.

It was Matt and Michael's birthday (twins). They'd turned eight.

Besides getting the kids some cones, I decided to tell Matt and Michael (and the rest of the kids) a "special story" for their birthday.

Now although I'm not Garrison Keilor of NPR *Prairie Home Companion* fame, I can hold my own when it comes to storytelling.

And this particular afternoon I decided to tell them a story about a "big blue penguin" in Antarctica (and this was well before I knew anything about the Bluffton/Antarctica connection, *I swear*) that only two people, me being one of them, had seen.

The kids, who were mostly six and seven, were rapt, eyes wide, hanging on every word as I described the penguin being *"even larger than the building we were in!"*

And what's more, the penguin was able to hold back gigantic ice shelves, catch whales with one fin, slide down glaciers for fun… when Matt said:

"Mr. Schriner, I don't think I believe this."

Apparently at age eight you start to stop "believing."

With Matt being one of the 'kid authorities' in the neighborhood by virtue of his age, I could now see questioning looks starting up among the rest.

I had to quickly save the moment.

So I turned to an older Bluffton couple at the next table, who I'd noticed were listening to the story as well.

Addressing the woman first, I said:

"Ma'am, you've heard of the big blue penguin, haven't you?" Wink.

After hesitating for a moment (and apparently a devout church member), she finally stammered: "Well, I, I'm not, I mean…"

Quickly, and imploringly, I turned to her husband (who apparently doesn't go to church as much).

He, quite convincingly I might add, said:

"*Oh yeah,* I saw a PBS special about that penguin just the other night!"

Bingo!

The kids, including Matt, were instantly transfixed.

I went on for quite a while with more big penguin 'tall, *real* tall, tales,' then ended by offering to take the kids down to Antarctica, the next day, to search for the Big Blue Penguin.

Needless to say, they all rushed home and started to pack (warm clothes, boots, everything). Then the more geography-minded of the kids rushed off to ask their parents where Antarctica was on the map

After a few calls from these same neighborhood parents, with the whole thing getting quickly out of hand, I had to fess up to Liz just exactly what I had done.

Her response, like at other times when I've done stupid stuff, was an exacerbated look and the rhetorical question:

"You *didn't?*"

And, as I always astutely reply at these times, I, rather red-faced, said:

"I did."

Chapter 34

Public Enemy #1

Speaking of 'tall tales,' or rather 'true tales'…

According to many around here, the most infamous day in Bluffton history was the day famed bank robber John Dillinger robbed Bluffton's Citizen's National Bank on Aug. 14, 1933. (I still contend the most infamous day occurred several years earlier -- the day Coach Burcky came up with "the beaver" idea.)

Anyway, the Dillinger bank robbery was such a big thing that they *still* talk about it, and in a rather weird, folklore type of way. Some even seem a little proud of it.

For instance, a *Bluffton News* headline on a summary of the story years later read: **The Day John Dillinger Robbed Our Bank.**

Our bank.

The reason, perhaps, for the pride, or at least lingering fascination, is that in an era (early '30s) of pretty notorious criminals, Pretty Boy Floyd, Machine Gun Kelly, Ma Barker… John Dillenger was Public Enemy #1 on FBI Director J. Edgar Hoover's list.

Hoover said: "He (Dillinger) was a cheap, boastful, selfish, tight-fisted, pug ugly…"

No love loss there.

Dillenger's bank robbery spree through the Midwest, committing the crimes often in "broad daylight" while being Houdini-like in avoiding capture, created a mystique that preceded him the day he came to Bluffton.

It was around noon, and a group of dapper dressed men walked in Citizen's National. While most of the men suspiciously milled about, Dillinger got in line.

Bluffton's Paul Faze was standing between Dillinger and the teller. He turned to see "...the coldest looking eyes I'd ever seen."

Faze did his banking business then left as Dillinger asked for change for a $5 bill. While the teller was getting the change, Dillinger pulled a gun.

The men rushed the counter and started putting the loot in a sack, while the bank personnel were ordered to lie on the floor. (The take this day would be $2,100 – which, it was noted, was insured by "burglary insurance.")

As the hoist was going on, the unexpected happened.

In probably the most self-evident (and overwritten) statement to ever appear in a newspaper, *Bluffton News* editor C.A. Biery wrote:

"The strident clanging of the gong outside the (bank) building on Church St. gave the first public intimation that something was awry in the bank."

Thanks Sherlock.

With the gong now "stridently clanging," the robbers dashed out of the bank firing their guns, although no one was injured and only one store window was broken.

They then hopped in the getaway car, "motor running" of course, and as Bluffton filling station operator Harold Montgomery reported, in what has to be the second most self-evident thing that has ever run in a newspaper, the men "...appeared to be in great haste."

Didn't even stop for some free air, nothing.

Note: John Dillinger was apprehended that year in Dayton and brought back here to Allen County Jail to await trial. However, he was "sprung" by a group of his buddies who shot up the jail. The Oct. 26, 1933 *Bluffton News* reported on the notorious criminal's jail break, on the guns that blazed, on the dramatic earlier town bank robbery that led to it all... and boxed right above this story's headline, in rather large, bold type was: **Bluffton: A Good Place To Live.**

Composition-wise, perhaps in this instance, oh, a case of bad placement.

And, ultimately, it would be a 'bad place' (back alley in Chicago) that Dillinger would find himself in not long after when a "Federal hit squad" gunned him down.

Chapter 35

Historical Society, and a 'Wisp of a Yodel'

Speaking of area history…

The Bluffton-Pandora Historical Society tries to keep local history alive and vital so there's a strong sense of heritage and connection to the past here.

Generally on the first Saturday in October (unless that day is BC's Homecoming), the Historical Society puts on a Fall Heritage Festival at the "old Schumacher House." The house was built in 1843 as the second dwelling in a new Swiss Mennonite settlement here.

Historical Society spokesperson Ann Hilty said spaces between the rough cut timber were filled in with a mixture of mud and straw. (Now there's a surface I'd like to see Dale try to 'hide his brush strokes' on.)

The Heritage Festival features demonstrations of traditional crafts and working methods: baking bread in an open brick oven, woodworking, blacksmithing, quilting, soap making – and anything else local people can add. Ann said there are also horse wagon rides for children, folk music and more.

Over the years, the Historical Society has published several books on local history. One book about life in the Bluffton and Pandora community between 1877 and 1910 is titled: *Life in the Bluffton and Pandora Community, 1877-1910.*

Imaginative titles must just be a part of Bluffton's history.

The following is an excerpt from the Historical Society
book, as reported in the Sept. 17, 1903 *Bluffton News*:

"Mr. Fred Rohrer... editor of the *Berne Witness* (a
newspaper in an Indiana Mennonite settlement) had his
home dynamited last Wednesday night, with the purpose,
undoubtedly, to kill him." [The newspaper had gotten behind an initiative to keep the town "dry," or alcohol free.
Incidentally, the murder attempt failed.]

Another part of Bluffton's history is the Historical
Society's "Swiss Day" held at Bluffton College every
June. Dinner and presentations about Switzerland high-
light the event.

Ann said, for instance, BC art Professor Gregg
Luginbuhl showed slides that chronicled his recent "ge-
nealogical journey" to Switzerland to see the sights of
his ancestors. (I told Liz that I *thought* I had discerned
an "Alps doodle," even the wisp of a yodel, in the professor's *First Last Draft* sculpture. She asked if my
Columbia Supremo blend coffee was "dry.")

Every year the Historical Society celebrates the
area's heritage even more with a "New Year Reception"
display of newly acquired tools, textile artifacts, old
photographs...at the Mennonite Memorial Home.

Chapter 36

Bluffton Seniors

Speaking of places for seniors…

One of the bullets fired by the Dillinger boys that day in Bluffton grazed the building that's now the home of the Bluffton Senior Center.

Essential to the "quality of life" in any community is how area seniors continue to be involved in the flow of life.

Bluffton Senior Center director Rosemary Meyer said the Center here is unusual in that it is almost totally self-supported, they take no state or federal funds.

Rosemary said they want to be free to pray, or do other things, that might be constricted if the Center was supported by the government.

The Senior Center derives income from local fund-raising, donations to memorial funds and from the arts and crafts members make. In addition, the Senior Center partners with the local Lions Club, and the United Way, in working on fundraisers for other causes.

The Senior Center also hosts Bible studies, dances, men's and women's discussion groups, a monthly potluck. At last months potluck, a Senior Center Bluffton couple showed slides from a recent trip to Alaska – yet another "cold place."

(See, what am I tellin' ya about those subliminal "Constellation Earth" sculpture messages. In fact, I don't think anybody here even goes to Florida anymore.)

Rosemary said it is essential seniors are able to socialize and continue to feel productive. And "we don't want to see the generations separated," she added, explaining the seniors particularly love to interact with children.

Bear Paw Quilt

And it was Liz and our Sarah and Joseph who, one day, stopped in to help some elderly women at the Center with a quilt they were making.

As they talked, Sarah particularly developed an interest in quilting. And when she saw the book: *The Bear Claw Quilt* at the Mennonite Church Library she asked Mom for it.

Upon reading the book, they found, serendipitously enough, the author was from right here in Bluffton, and she was currently staying at the First Mennonite Memorial Nursing Home, one of three nursing home / assisted living facilities in town.

Sarah and Liz trekked out to the Home, where the author, Barbara Smucker, asked Sarah and Liz if they would read her her book. Liz relayed it was such a special moment watching both Mrs. Smucker's animation, and Sarah's fascination, in their time together.

Senior Concerns

First Mennonite Church members, and others, support the Mennonite Memorial Home and Maple Crest Home through donations and ministries to help the elderly there.

Claude Boyer, president of First Mennonite's Senior Concerns Committee, said church teams regularly visit at the nursing homes and with others who may be homebound. (Each person will be visited at least once a month, birthday cards are sent, and the teams regularly meet to strategize about other ways to help.)

In addition, the church van, equipped with the latest in handicap equipment, picks seniors up for Sunday services, and other church functions. The driver: Dale Way.

Claude said current church statistics show that there are more than 150 people in First Mennonite's congregation who are over 65 years of age.

What's more, once someone has "passed," First Mennonite still doesn't stop helping.

Note: In 1991, Bluffton College established an "Institute for Learning in Retirement." The classes include religion, science, computer, literature, music, gourmet foods (macaroni, I've heard, is not on the menu), politics... almost all participants are over 55 years old, with many in their 70s and 80s.

Chapter 37

'Quality of Death'

You know, I've talked a lot about the quality of life, but what about the 'quality of death?'

A Bluffton friend of mine, Matt Meyer, said he recently attended a mall show in Lima that included a cemetery booth. He said he was told the "cheapest way to go" with a cemetery spot is a vault in a mausoleum: $3,000. (I'll tell ya, for 3,000 bucks, I'd want a vault with a view.)

Matt said he also learned at the show that an average burial in America now costs between $8,000 to $15,000 (plot, casket, funeral home costs…).

Neil Kehler, who helps coordinate a "Casket Ministry" at First Mennonite, told me an average "on the market" casket costs about $4,300.

An "average Joe" math word problem:

Homes for the Poor, an international aid agency out of Deerfield Beach, Florida, says it can build a rather nice home for a fairly big homeless family in Haiti, or any number of other Third World countries, for $2,000. (Same price as the homes in Afghanistan the BC students were raising money for.)

On the lower end, say funeral expenses for a typical American come to $10,000.

$10,000 divided by $2,000 = 5 (homes).

Back to the First Mennonite "Casket Ministry." Neil told me when someone passes in the church, congregation "carpenter hobbyists" build a nice casket out of oak or cherry wood, with other church members lining it with satin. Cost: $300.

$4,300 (average market casket) minus $300 = 2 homes.

First Mennonite's Andy Chappell Dick then told me burial plots at their church cemetery are free, $200 for a non-member. (I asked Andy the criteria for a non-member. He winked and said: "Oh, we just have to like you." Mennonites like everybody.)

$4,000 (average cemetery plot, no view) minus zero = 2 more homes.

Also, my wife Liz said she just read where some Amish and Mennonites do the "viewing" in their homes and have a potluck. (First Mennonite is always having potlucks, for anything.)

Home viewing and potluck = 1 home.

Summation:

If you're buried through First Mennonite, your Last Will & Testament could, conceivably, provide for the housing of: up to five families in the Third World.

Chapter 38

Highlander Grogg and
'That's All Folks…'

Speaking of the end….

You know how I said at the beginning of the book that Bluffton is the best town in America.

Well, I just *said* that -- to get your attention.

There actually could be towns out there that are better. (Plus, obviously, I don't think we're going to carry the whole country just on Bluffton's 1,300 registered voters.)

I also said Bluffton was best because I live here, and you like to think the town you live in is the best; just like people in Yellow Springs, Ohio, like to think their town is the best; or people in Rising Sun, Maryland, like to think their town is the best; or, if you live in Klamath Falls, Oregon, and think your town is the best – have another double Espresso. I've been there.

A town is what you make of it, for worse, for better, for best.

And if your town has any "quality of life" stuff that's better, or even that we don't have, write us. Or better yet, write Wendy or Dale.

If your town doesn't have some of the "quality of life" stuff Bluffton has, feel free to use the ideas. We don't have a patent, or want one.

Or if you need a closer look at the projects in action here, come.

Bluffton or Pebble Beach?

You know how I also said at the beginning that Bluffton isn't exactly considered a "tourist Mecca?" Well, after writing this book, I'm convinced, that while not the Hawaiian Islands, Bluffton would be a great vacation spot.

If you've decided to camp at nearby Twin Lakes Good Sam Park, I'm sure Bill Keeney will let you borrow his lantern. Just allow time (about a day), to get it lit.

Or you could, for instance, stay at one of the two rooms at Bluffton's Victorian-style The Lamplight Bed & Breakfast. (If they're full, there are Comfort and Knights Inns out by the I-75 exit, surrounded by Burger King, McDonald's, Subway... and the biggest fireworks store in Ohio. Well, you'll probably want to celebrate after being here.)

And staying with the fireworks theme, if you've got "money to burn," I'd recommend starting off with a trip to one of the town's three hardware stores for one of those six-in-one screw drivers. They come in green, and yellow – for those of you with yellow shoe laces.

Then, perhaps, you might want to "square dance" about the rest of downtown for awhile, walking the antique malls, browsing the used book store and stopping in at the meat market for a loaf of Amish bread and some slices of Italian turkey (my favorite). For desert, I recommend heading down to The Depot for a cone. Who knows, you just might happen across a story teller spell binding a group of kids. Caution: No matter what the story – you have to go along with it.

If spectator's sports are your thing, the town of Bluffton's website: www.blufftonohio.org has a weekly list of college events, including games. Or, stop down to the Bluffton Family Recreation Center, I'm sure the Spartans could always use even more supporters.

If you lean more toward participatory sports, and you've "got game," or for that matter just have an alarm clock, we're always down at BC's basketball court Mondays and Fridays.

Or Bluffton has a nice 18-hole golf club, which, in the tradition of other local well thought out names, is called the: Bluffton Golf Club. While not Pebble Beach, there are some challenging holes. And if the wind is blowing just right, and you squint hard enough, the waving of the surrounding wheat fields reminds one of the Pacific's waves rolling in at Pebble. (OK, well maybe sort of.)

Look for the helicopter blades

Speaking of interpretive scenes, after your round of golf, you might want to stop out at the college to see the "dog/monkey" piece, and tour the rest of the Centennial Sculpture Garden – which is just down the path from BC's bookstore where I'm sure you'll want to stop in to get some perfunctory clothing item that has "the beaver" on it.

Following this, a trip over a wooden foot bridge to the college's Peace Center may be in order, to view the striking art and take in a sense of peace, diversity and social justice. And then, being steeped in, say, this social justice, you might want to look for Jean-Paul Tiendrebeogo and give him some money to take back to Burkina-Faso.

Or instead, you may want to look for a BC student just back from a cross cultural trip to Northern Ireland.

In that case, once you've found him/her, pull up a couple "peace stone" seats and learn about what people in Ireland are doing to keep the "green, green grass" of peace alive there.

If it's a Thursday, after this conversation, I recommend heading one block east for the Chappell-Dick's potluck, "everyone welcome." And while you're there, ask Andy to take you to the shop out back to watch him saw something without electricity, BC artist Bill Millmine influence.

And if you miss the potluck, and you find yourself hungry, you can always stop down at the hospital (whether you're sick, or not) for a 25 cent muffin. Although the kids and I decided not to tell you just exactly where the hospital is.

However, in the off chance you do find it (hint: look for the Life Flight helicopter blades), then it would be off to Common Grounds to wash the muffin(s) down with a steaming fresh cup of Highlander Grogg blend coffee.

While you're at the Cafe, stop in the back room, which is open to town groups for free, and which, once a week, or so, doubles as the informal "average Joe" campaign headquarters. (Have I mentioned it's a low budget campaign?)

Also, if I'm not there, check out the "average Joe" Presidential Library, which, by the way, doubles as BC's Musselman Library. I'm usually by the *National Geographics* brushing up on foreign affairs stuff. (Well, the Bluffton Girl Scouts only do that country display thing once a year, and they can't include *everywhere.)*

And on your way out of town, don't make the same mistake the Dillinger boys made. Stop and fill your tires up with some of the free air.

Also, if any of these tourism suggestions doesn't particularly suit you, just contact the Bluffton's Visitor's Bureau and ask for director (Are you ready for this?) Dale Way. (When asked what he does in his spare time, Dale said: "sleep.")

And if you want to combine the trip to Bluffton with one to Antarctica, or even around the world, talk to BC's administration office. It's reported, as an alumni donation, Hugh Downs has given the college his frequent flier miles.

Note: While I could have written even much more about Bluffton, I ran out of Common Grounds coffee flavors. When I got to something called "Highlander Grogg" (which I haven't had the guts to try yet), you had to know I'd reached the end.

Almost.

Chapter 39

Painter's Plus Postscript

"*Eat a Peach*,"
Almond Brothers revisited

Speaking of Dale Way, and unsavory cuisine…

Another, what I'd have to believe an anomaly among handyman crews is a 9 a.m. – on the dot – Painter's Plus tradition. That's when the 5-minute "Writer's Almanac" segment comes on our NPR affiliate station out of Toledo.

Everything stops.

Big empty plastic paint tubs are turned over, step ladders, tool boxes, or whatever's handy, are pulled up as seats to make a circle around the radio.

Hosted by Garrison Keillor, gentle piano "Writer's Almanac" theme music preludes a list of famous, and not so famous, authors and poets "born on this day." This includes works they were known for and sometimes a brief snatch from their life.

These reports are often accompanied by appreciative Painter's Plus literary circle: "*Ah,* I didn't know that about Thoreau…" or, "No wonder e.e. cummings strove for the unconventional," or…

As an aside, during these -- I don't want to

cheapen the experience by saying "coffee breaks," as much as they were -- "literary interludes," the owner of a place we were working on, or a plumbing crew, or flooring crew (like "Big Roger" Edward's)... would happen by.

They would often then momentarily take in the scene, literally, or figuratively (if you'll allow me), raise an eyebrow, scratch a head, and move on -- I'm sure thinking: *'What the heck...'*

But we wouldn't move, waiting in anticipation for the "Poem of the Day."

Picking, again, a poet whose birthday is that day, Garrison will, in fluctuating tone and accent, almost reverently recite long flowing sonnets, short poignant haiku, and other verse, some rhyming, some not.

We always listen in silence.

After a pause following the poem, the theme music will again begin to play and Garrison will say who Writer's Almanac is "brought to you by..."

And at last, he will end with, always ends with: "Be well. Do good work. And keep in touch."

Now, instead of going off to immediately "do good work," the Painter's Plus crew stays put to "do good interpretation."

For the next five minutes, or longer (it varies), we discuss meter, cadence, I think even once someone (not this "average Joe") mentioned the quality of a poem's "iambic pentameter." Then we moved into what the poem symbolized to us.

Example:

It was a hot July morning in Bluffton and we were all outside painting a fence when Writer's Almanac came on. The poem this day was, appropriately enough, about a steamy summer day in Georgia.

While I can't remember the poet's name, or even the title now, I do remember, vividly, it was about a day in the South when the air hangs heavy, like the ripe Georgia peaches hang heavy on the tree.

The poet stops to notice these peaches, filmed with a light coating of dust, kicked up over time by wheels and wind from a nearby dirt back road.

In the moment, and after a rather descriptive, poignant build-up, the poet plucks the peach (notice the consonance there), purposely does not wipe off the dust because it is as much a part of the scene, as the rest of the slower paced Southern rural culture, and finally, and with abandon:

…bites deep into the succulence.

Afterward in the 'circle,' Dale and I launched into a series of deep analysis, as Liz, who would occasionally work with us, and who believed that poetry analysis (like hospitals being meant only for the sick), should be better left to English professors, sat quietly.

I said I was particularly struck by the poem's Southern imagery and the rich languidness of the scene – in contrast to the ever increasing, frenetic pace of contemporary America. (I've been spending a lot of time at Andy Chappell-Dick's workshop lately.)

Dale then said he found the piece stirring as well, and what impacted him was the final line when the poet, with abandon, reaches for, and bites into, the "dusty peach." He said he saw that as a metaphor for grabbing for life in all its gritty fullness – not being afraid to risk.

Then, out of the blue, Liz said, almost in passing (*Like it was no big deal!*): "I used to work on a farm in New Zealand that had a peach grove. And I would often eat dusty peaches."

Awed, almost reverent silence followed.

Then:

"You've actually *eaten* dusty peaches?" I asked.

Liz nodded.

Perhaps it was envy, perhaps it was merely too much emersion in symbolism, maybe it was even just one too many store bought 'polished peaches'; but whatever it was, Dale abruptly retreated from poetic analysis, and passionately exclaimed:

"I just wish I had one of those dusty peaches to bite into right now!"

Time passed.

It was August and the Thursday night pot luck gang was preparing a surprise birthday party for Dale this evening. It was to be a gala gathering.

In cogitating about what I could buy Dale for under a dollar (have I mentioned... yeah I have...), it, at last, came to me in what I'd like to think was the collective wisdom, and frugality, of every starving poet that has gone before.

I mounted my bike and headed to the Dave's Market produce section, where I, with much searching, looked for the most "succulent" peach I could find, on sale.

I then headed to the *Ye Old Haus of Cards* where they quite graciously (but admittedly with a few smirks) found some white tissue paper and a white gift box that fit the peach perfectly.

One problem: The peach was yet decidedly too 'polished,'

So I was then off to find our Joseph.

In the Schriner clan, if there is an expert on dirt, mud, and things of that sort, it's Joseph.

As a preface to the next part, you know how I've said Bluffton is the "best" in a lot of different categories? Well, I have to admit in the soil category, let's just say the glacier wasn't generous. In fact, at an agricultural seminar at First Mennonite the other day, a local farmer explained the soil here is about an even mix of dirt and clay.

And this combination gets pretty hard around August.

Now being in step with others in Bluffton. who are not using chemical fertilizers, we have "learned to love bare spots" of this soil mix in our back yard. And it is to one of these bare spots that I directed Joseph to go to "lightly dust" the peach.

So off he headed with his toy yellow metal "big digger," on a mission.

Finding the spot, Joseph began scraping and digging, digging and scraping, occasionally mixing in some spittle to loosen the ground up.

He then 'smeared' the peach ("lightly dust" being a nuance lost on Joseph) with this concoction. And, as I'm sure BC artist Bill Millmine felt when he finished "cutting" his picture, Joseph, beaming, brought his 'art' back to his father.

Since the peach was still somewhat recognizable as a peach, and thinking Dale would merely make the cognitive connection (notice again the consonance) to the poem, smile and merely set it aside, I said:

"Thanks Joseph, it looks great!"

That night

Amidst the song, gaiety and gift giving, Dale, at last, got to "the white box." Carefully he unwrapped the paper, opened the lid and crinkled the tissue back, revealing: the peach.

An instant smile of recognition (Dale never forgets anything), came to his face.

However, instead of then just appreciatively setting

the peach aside, Dale "the actor," who sees all of life as a stage, found this the perfect time for a cameo – and quickly moved the peach to his lips.

Before I could shout: **STOP!**, Dale bit deep with "abandon," and began to chew.

"*Ew,* I can't believe you did that!" I managed.

"Did what?" He asked, the smile then starting to go, and the 'chewing with abandon,' being replaced with what can be best described as 'crunching with caution.'

Right at that moment, and actually quite apt for that moment, I'm sure Dale wished he had some Southern Pecan Pie coffee blend (I'd forgotten that one) to wash down the clay.

Meanwhile, Joseph, who has eaten his share of clay, dirt, mud, and an occasional worm, stared transfixed.

He now had a new adult "Bluffton hero."

End Note(s)

Speaking, again, of Bluffton heroes…

OK, I will shame-facedly, or sort of shame-facedly, fess up.

There are, in fact, some Bluffton College track shoes among the Sports Hall of Fame displays here.

In order to keep the "beaver/track" thing going, I couldn't let on.

If the truth be known, however, in recent history BC track and field teams won the Heartland Conference in 1992, '94 and '95 – on the strength, I'm sure, of the shot putters and discuss throwers.

Wow, I just can't stop doing that.

GO BEAVERS!

Yet a New Type of "Diversity"

A recent edition of the *Bluffton News* included a letter to the editor by John Timmerman from the "Center for UFO Studies." He explained a Bluffton woman had recently reported a UFO sighting (true story), and was exhorting others in the town who may have seen the phenomenon to contact him.

Out the back window of her home one night, the woman reported seeing what looked like a space craft with extremely bright lights.

With the naked eye, because the craft was at such a high altitude, the woman wasn't able to make out much more.

Luckily, some Bluffton College astronomy class students were out with their telescopes that night. Seeing the unusual light, they turned from Jupiter to the direction the light was coming from.

And they saw that it was indeed a modern-looking space ship coated in a bright alloy – sporting, of all things, Betel Guese (again, pronounced "Beetle Juice") Colony colors.

From the "arm pit" of the galaxy, to the "jewel." Who could blame them?

The craft hovered just long enough to find both rooms at the Lamplight B&B ("Reservations appreciated.") were taken.

The aliens then briefly made "contact" with BC's "Constellation Earth" sculpture.

Then they were off, like a (speed of light) shot.

A local ham radio operator, who had just had his unit fixed at Norm's Electronics in downtown Bluffton, picked up a faint radio transmission.

Mysteriously, the 'Beetles' had decided to deviate from there intended flight plan back to Betel Guese, opting, instead -- to circle the galaxy. After this, they, even more inexplicably, had decided to winter at Pluto, the "frozen planet," where the sun *never* shines and temperatures reach as low as -235 degrees Celsius.

However, the radio operator also picked up the aliens did intend to come back to Bluffton in June to see if they could purchase some fuzzy dice for their craft at the Festival of Wheels.

In the ensuing days, as the story leaked out – unlike the tremendous stir created in Roswell, New Mexico, in the wake of their "UFO incident" – Blufftonites pretty much took the news of the sighting in stride.

The general feeling was this would just merely take the town to the next level of "diversity."

However, there was a stir at Bluffton College as administrators hurriedly met to see if there was a way to stretch the budget to include: "inter-galactic scholarships."

GO BEETLES!

Hey wait, how about: **"Nothing Runs Like a Beetle!"?**
No, that won't work either.

Odd note: While at the hospital cafeteria the other day for a muffin, I mentioned the Bluffton UFO sighting to one of the medical staff there. She said she hadn't seen the initial report in the *Bluffton News*, "…but funny you're mentioning this." She said she lives in a rural area on the outskirts of Bluffton, and the other night her and her sons were startled while looking out their back window. She said while she couldn't determine the source, inexplicably out in the field was a pattern of ul-tra-bright lights. She continued there are no roads anywhere near where the lights were, and she was con-vinced they weren't coming from a conventional (read: "earthling") vehicle. In fact, the lights were unlike any she'd seen before.

Yep, word about Bluffton is getting out. *Way* out.

You might want to consider making your "reserva-tions" early.

"Average Joe" final thought:

(I bet you're thinking this book is *never* going to end...)

While Hugh Downs was in Antarctica walking around the world in "24 (time zone) steps," if one of his crew on the other side of the circle at any point would have rung Hugh on his cell phone – would that have been a long distance call?

Well, somebody's got to think about that stuff.

Schriner family (photo courtesy of *Fremont Messenger* newspaper)

About the author: When they are not out campaigning on the back roads of America, "average Joe" Schriner and his family reside in Bluffton, Ohio - one of their favorite towns. Besides being an independent presidential candidate, Joe is also an avid Bluffton, Ohio supporter. So avid, in fact, that the *Findlay Courier* newspaper recently reported that in one of Joe's local campaign speeches, he said one of the first things he'll do when he gets to D.C. is: "replace the bald eagle with: 'the beaver.' "

- "Average Joe" is also the author of the book: *Back Road to the White House.* (For more on the campaign, see: **www.voteforjoe.com**)

To order more copies of *America's Best Town (Bluffton, Ohio 45817),* or *Back Road to the White House,* see following pages.

Order form

America's Best Town
(Bluffton, Ohio 45817)

$14.95 plus $4.50 Shipping & Handling

**Available Through Bookstores Everywhere
or by ordering through Llumina Press**

Llumina Press
8055 W. McNab Road
Tamarac, Florida 33021
(866) 229-9244
www.llumina.com

Quantity:_____ Price:_____

Name:_____

Address:_____

_____

Phone:_____

Email:_____

Another book by "Average Joe" Schriner:

Back Road to the White House
(Hamburg Press)
…A phenomenal true story of grassroots politics.

Against all odds, and then some, an "average guy" from the Midwest does the unthinkable. He runs for president of the United States. No party machine. No big money. Just a dream – and an old van.

What they are saying about Joe:

"I'm in awe…" Doug Raymond, Straight Talk Radio host, Morehead City, N.C.

"…he seems to make a lot more sense than most politicians I try not to listen to." Steve Zender, Editor, The Progressor-Times Newspaper, Carey, Ohio.

Available Through Bookstores Everywhere